MW00932171

"Why Should I?"

Jack Moore knew he had it all: devoted wife, talented kids, Purple Heart award, Hall of Fame career. And a pacemaker. And Alzheimer's disease. And colon cancer. When a doctor recommended surgery to treat the cancer and maybe add a few years to this good life, Jack's response was, "Why should I?"

It's always three little words that set a story into motion. Jack's family and friends purchased plane tickets, cancelled plans and quietly closed their laptops. In cities around the globe, they packed for indefinite travel and said goodbye to families of their own.

Soon, a dozen highly accomplished professionals were crowded into an overheated two-room apartment in the middle of a frigid Minnesota December, staring at one another and wondering, "Now what?"

HOSPICE

Isn't a Place

It's People

By
Julie Desmond

With Contributions from
the Moore Family

Illustrations by
Emily L. Moore & Robert H. Moore

Hospice Isn't a Place; It's People by Julie Desmond
Copyright © 2014 by Julie Desmond.

All rights reserved. This book is protected under the copyright laws of the United States of America. Reproduction or unauthorized use of the material or artwork herein is prohibited except with the express written permission of the Author. For information and permission, contact the author.

Illustrations, poetry, and prose contributed by **MOORE family** members, including excerpts from **WE NEVER SAID GOODBYE by JACK I. MOORE** (New York: CGM, 2013) and **www.weneversaidgoodbye.com**, used by permission. All rights belong to individual contributors.

ISBN-13: 978-1491244173 ISBN-10: 1491244178 www.hospicepeople.org

Gail Wenner, "**Why the Willette Room**?" *Circles of Care,* September 2008. Used by permission of the author.

EASY TO LOVE (from "Anything Goes")
Words and Music by **COLE PORTER** © 1936 CHAPPELL & CO., INC.
Copyright Renewed and Assigned to ROBERT H. MONTGOMERY,
Trustee of the COLE PORTER MUSICAL & LITERARY PROPERTY TRUSTS.
Publication and Allied Rights Assigned to CHAPPELL & CO., INC.
All Rights Reserved. Used by Permission of ALFRED MUSIC.

THE POEMS OF EMILY DICKINSON: VARIORUM EDITION, edited by Ralph W. Franklin, Cambridge, Mass.: The Belknap Press of Harvard University Press, Copyright © 1998 by the President and Fellows of Harvard College. Copyright © 1951, 1955, 1979, 1983 by the President and Fellows of Harvard College.

Scripture texts in this work are taken from the *New American Bible, revised edition* © 2010, 1991, 1986, 1970 Confraternity of Christian Doctrine, Washington, D.C., and are used by permission of the copyright owner. All Rights Reserved. No part of the New American Bible may be reproduced in any form without permission in writing from the copyright owner.

TAPS sheet music: This file is made available under the Creative Commons CC0 1.0 Universal Public Domain Dedication.

The Cracked Pot is a traditional Indian folktale, retold by **Kevin Kling.** Used with his permission.

Elizabeth Alexander, excerpt from "**Ars Poetica #100: I Believe**" from *Crave Radiance: New and Selected Poems 1990-2010.* Copyright © 2005 by Elizabeth Alexander. Reprinted with the permission of The Permissions Company, Inc., on behalf of Graywolf Press, Minneapolis, Minnesota, www.graywolfpress.org.

Quote from **Mother Teresa**: Teresa; González-Balado, José Luis, **Mother Teresa: In My Own Words** (Liguori: Liguori Publications, 1997). Print.

"**Facts & Figures: Hospice Care in America**" published by National Hospice and Palliative Care Organization, www.nhpco.org.

In affectionate memory of Dad

Jack I. Moore
12/26/1922–12/19/2012

Dedicated to Mom, Emily Moore, who, during Dad's hospice, stayed beside our father on the big bed and held his hand and listened when he tried to speak. She didn't hear the impassioned conversations of her adult children in the next room. She didn't read our searching, serious, and spirited e-mail; she didn't referee our disagreements. For many days, surrounded by family, she didn't see anyone but her husband. As it should be.

Take Care of Your Father

when he is OLD;

grieve him not as long as he lives.

Even if his mind fail, be considerate of him;

revile him not all the days of his life;

kindness to a father will not be forgotten,

firmly planted against the debt of your sins—

a house raised in justice to you.

Sirach 4:14

Contents

Introduction: Mancala

Before Dad died, he said that he had to go. He had "things to do," and he had "plans." Several weeks later, he tracked me down and let me know that his plans included me, and that I'd better get started. He reached me on my smartphone. That's what I realize now, although I did not see it that way at the time: the day I read the message, Dad had been gone two months already.

I have a sister who spends more time on the phone with psychics than siblings. She really believes in the connection between here and whatever comes after. Me, not so much. When I die, I want to be doing otherworldly things; I don't want to hang around here haunting people. But can a message come through from the wherever? I think it can.

Dad liked "smart." He used to sit at the head of the fourteen-foot conference table in our family's kitchen and announce, "Let's have a quiz."

While Mom rattled away at the dinner dishes, the eleven or so children around the table eagerly showed off their smarts by finding the square root of some number or by spelling a complicated word like b-e-a-u-t-i-f-u-l. Dad's quiz show had no format. There was no prize. The winner was the last one left at the table. Usually, it was my MENSA brother, Terry. After Terry correctly answered five or six in a row, the rest of the family gradually lost interest; one at a time we would ask, "May I please be excused?" and skip away to the rest of our lives.

Dad embraced smart. He took risks with innovative technologies such as reel-to-reel tape, FM stereo radio, and satellite television, back when these were innovative devices. He liked Cadillacs. He liked computers. He handily juggled the three "shooters" that managed his TV and its components. He even called his granddaughter's violin a "machine." And he delighted in the concept of smartphones, although he never had one of his own. He would watch someone tapping away on a tiny handheld box and ask, "What are you doing with that?" Dad instilled curiosity in all of us, and we went out into the world seeking smart things for ourselves.

When Dad knew he was dying, he knew that his People—his wife, his kids—would have his back. He knew his People would come up with creative and effective solutions to resolve whatever problems arose. He trusted us to come through for him the way he had always come through for us. Ultimately, it was smarts that got us through Dad's Alzheimer's disease, cancer diagnosis, and hospice care. Smartphones, smart technologies, smart ideas, smart mouths... these all came into play.

But smart can startle sometimes. A person can be searching through the trash on her smartphone and see a list of messages, each prefaced by a notation such as, "This message sent 61 days ago." It happened this way to me one perfectly ordinary winter afternoon. I remembered that I hadn't circled back to that old friend who wanted to get together around the holidays. I searched for her name in my phone and reread our conversations, including this message, sent sixty-one days earlier:

> **Yesterday buried my dad Too wrecked to go out Maybe tomorrow**

That note brought everything back; my grief was still raw, the tears behind my eyes were still hot, and the elephant settled on my heart weighed as much as it had two months before.

I swallowed hard, copied and pasted that message into a new e-mail form, and tapped out a poem to my siblings, as we'd all done from time to time. There is no time or space to edit thoughts or poems composed on a tiny keyboard. Think. Type. Send. Then quietly skip away to the rest of our lives.

That day, I set my grief loose through smart technology, knowing it would arrive in every sibling's e-mail box simultaneously. That day, I spread my sadness thin, asking each of my siblings to carry some on my behalf. Another day, they would spread theirs, until the loss would become a layer of thicker skin across everyone's hearts, fusing all of us closer together. When we were kids, if something hurt, Dad would say, "That smarts." Yes, smart smarts. Go ahead, roll your eyes; he'd love that.

Long after day 61 had come and gone, I realized that the poem I wrote that day was the beginning of Dad's plan for me. Reaching through a smartphone was his way of saying, "Remember my story; share my story. Help someone else. You can. You are smart. You can do this."

For the guy who always said, "You should be filling wastebaskets!" I have done so. What's left is his story, at last.

Mancala: Many Hands, Many Voices

This message sent 61 days ago:

Yesterday, buried my dad Too wrecked to go out Maybe tomorrow

The game begins against our will

61 days ago?
So, 62 days ago
I stood frozen over my father's
casket.

Tinted glass stones
slip with clicks into
shallow bowls smoothed
Into a bamboo board
Click click

And, 63 days ago, we calculated
prayer cards, coffee cups and
parking spaces
and whistled, He would have
been
90 today

12 bowls, six and six, running
the length of the board
troughs on either end

12 days before that,
a 700 mile countdown
across 5 states
a race to spend
5 eternal days dividing 6 hour
shifts,
figuring 3 people per shift can
sleep 4 hours each
Measuring
2.5 every 2 hours something
else every 6

and now we look up
one fist suspended above the
board

stones willing themselves
to fall

We heard,
had 11 children
married 56 years

handfuls of gems
shimmer in the light

click click clink click

We counted
spoonfuls of Popsicle
shirts cut up the back
beads on a rosary
stitches across a quilt
Counted breaths
and arpeggios of time between
breaths

click clink
A stone falls away
from the board

We counted on God

we gaze guiltily down

and on each other

at the piles of solid colors
glance up to catch a bird
flitting
outside the open window
under a vanishing sun
click click click

61 days?
70 days?
90 years?

Our game ends gently

Yesterday.

Part 1

Hospice Isn't a Place

Introduction to
Hospice, Death, and Dying

Doctor this. Doctor that. No matter.
You will go when you wish.
At your signal, we will get the window
And no darkness shall follow

What Death Looks Like

It Begins with a Life

A cold windy evening in NE Minneapolis
She held him in her arms
Her firstborn
She kissed his head and whispered
Do you know how much we love you?
He moved his newborn lips as if to say Yes
She kissed him again
Do you know how much I love you?
He moved his newborn lips as if to say Yes
Time went on and he grew
He became a man—not an ordinary man
A great man—and she loved him
She reveled in watching him grow
He fell in love and became
A husband, father
As time went on, grandfather, great-grandfather
It was a cold, windy night in NE Minneapolis
She watched them as the love of his life
held him in her arms
She kissed his head
Do you know how much we love you?
Yes, he whispered quietly
Do you know how much I love you?
Yes, he whispered again
She kissed him and he exhaled
He walked to his mother, who held him in her arms.

-        Sharon

When the word HOSPICE enters the vocabulary, it arrives holding hands with that other word: DEATH. Most books about hospice, dying, and death cover the event in chronological order. Around chapter 9, for example, we find a list of the signs of death. Most curious people, even people who are not intimately affected by terminal illness but who are, perhaps, thinking about death or being trained to provide hospice care to others, will take the same approach to the literature. They scan the table of contents and flip first of all to the page that says, "Signs that death is approaching." Is this a testament to how crude our society has become? Or simply a desire to comprehend something entirely foreign? No matter. They read the list, seriously consider their own proximity to blue lips and rattling breaths, and they rank themselves.

"Here is where we are," they say. "We are eating, but we no longer care who wins the election. However, we do care about who wins the Super Bowl, so perhaps we are not shutting down altogether." They peer into the eyes and lips and fingernails of their loved one and beg to know, "When?" and "How long?"

Hospice care is partly about letting life take its natural course. In that spirit, this book will explain, first, what people want most to know. Allowing that every death is unique, much like every birth is unique, some traits are seen commonly by people who care for the dying.

This story is about one dad. So this book will share with you that our dad hit many of the expected milestones, but drifted among them, also. We saw his appetite diminish, until we discovered chocolate shakes—which he craved, enjoyed, and thanked us for, until just a day or two before his death. He lost interest in the outside world generally, but even through the veil of Alzheimer's disease, he still cared deeply about the presidential election, and about whether his grandson's hockey team won tournament games. Did his feet turn blue? A little, but never blue like a summer sky. We counted his breaths and the spaces between them like notes and spaces on ancient sheet music, the kind that needs to be handled tenderly; the kind you expect will disintegrate in your hands if you turn the pages too often. We wondered if he could understand us when his eyes no longer opened, and we knew by the REM behind his closed lids that when my mother spoke, he heard. A furrow above his browline, a number eleven cutting into his forehead, indicated pain sometimes, and we were able to help with that. By the slightest twitch of his hand, we knew that he knew we were there.

What should we watch for, people wonder, when the end is across the table from us, rapping its fingers on the bare wood? When the only other sound is the tick tick tick of a clock or the deafening pound of hearts or the scream of the wind haunting like a phantom outside the rattling window?

Step away from your loved one for a moment; the answer is not under his closed eyelids, nor in his mottled skin, nor even in the creamy blue tint in his creamy white toes. Look toward the doorway. Then you will know that today is the day.

Beware the gathering. Not because a nurse says, "It's coming," but because death is a supermagnet drawing the hearts of so many people toward one another. In our case, a few hours before Dad's death, every kid in the family, plus a couple of grandkids, found themselves drawn by a power seemingly not their own into Mom and Dad's apartment on the Memory floor of their senior-centric home at River Village.

"We should have shifts," said my practical sister Penny. Her wild brown mane was piled into an unruly but practical bun. Penny could be deeply thoughtful and knee-slappingly hilarious in the same breath, usually not meaning to be either.

"We do have shifts," I reminded her.

"I mean, shifts when people are not allowed to come in. When we lock the door and the people scheduled to be outside have to go home and sleep or work or go to a bar or something."

"Except Virginia," said my sister Mickey, referring to a resident who wandered day and night on the Memory floor, likely scoping out new living arrangements, letting herself in when she found a door unlocked. Tall, direct and intent Mickey is one of those people who look out for people.

"Yeah, Virginia can come in," added my eldest brother, Rob. The joker took one look at our exhausted and gullible adult nephew, Cliff, whose huge black eyes were red rimmed from… from what? Lack of sleep? Tears? Six foot four, weighing in at 250 pounds, bawling like a baby… or like a guy who loves his dying grandpa. Rob gestured toward the door, "Cliffy, you know where Virginia is. Go get her."

We all gathered there the afternoon of the night my father died. If only we'd taken a picture. If only we'd thought of crowding up on the big bed and asking one of the nurses to snap a photo on one of our phones. There is no Moore family photo that includes every one of us kids along with both parents. This was our chance. What were we thinking? We weren't thinking. We were just doing. And we would have been missing our deceased brother, Jay, so perhaps that bird had already flown.

Here's the point: When everyone shows up, even though they know it could be a long week, even though they have horses to care for, depositions to reschedule, cigarettes to smoke outside - when everyone can think of no place better to be - then that is a sign that death is approaching. When people bring love and fear into a place, with the distinct absence of purpose outside of just being present, then something big is going on.

"Whose shift is it now?" Terry asked that afternoon.

"Mine," said deceptively little Lindy. Within the height of a gymnast, Lindy carries a great laugh and a huge personality. She has a knack for getting people to go along and so she is always willing to take charge.

"Then you give the meds," directed Terry, who believes he is in charge regardless of who is in any room, and usually he is right.

Lindy pulled herself up wearily and reached for one of the metal link chains hanging from the cuckoo clock perched above the square kitchen table which, cluttered with reading material, medical supplies, pop cans and other essentials, had been pushed out of the way, against the wall. She found a tiny silver key at the end of the chain and pulled it toward a white plastic medicine box on the table. She unlocked the box, lifted the lid, and peered inside. The key dangled from its chain, disappearing in the dim light among the clock's many silver threads. We all watched Lindy silently for one of those elongated moments as she remembered something, lowered the lid, and locked it again. The meds she needed were not in the box, but were already prepared in syringes on the counter.

When a person's mind is spinning, when someone is trying deeply to do only the right things, she will forget that the meds are no longer locked in their box. But she will remember after a minute and she will jot down the date, time and dosage; she will dispense the meds properly and life will go on for a while.

"Who's scheduled for tonight?" someone asked.

"I am," said a couple of us. Eventually, we on the night shift made the decision to leave for a while. It was a gamble. But there was a deep sentiment among us that we had completed our relationship with Dad, that every extra breath was a gift, and that if the angels came to take him and we were not all at his bedside to see him off, it would be all right and possibly even as it was meant to be. We would all be in our right places whenever it came to pass.

"Fine, fine," you say. "But how will we know? How will my family know? Scientifically?"

I'm getting to that. Following is a list of commonly accepted signs of a life wrapping itself up. Understand that this is not definitive, and it is not within any person's control. A life is a really big thing, no matter how long or short its span, and not having control is unnerving for those of us losing a piece of who we are.

There's a golf course just north of the Twin Cities called Bunker Hills. The majority of our summer weekends growing up were around that golf course, caddying or playing a round. In those days, some busy train tracks ran along the fourteenth fairway. We would stand at the tee box for minutes at a time, hearing the whistle and waiting for the train to pass before we teed off.

Death is like that. We stand and wait for the arriving train. We want to recognize a lonely, distant whistle. We want to feel the subtle tremble of the tracks and hear the muffled groan of a train's engine growing from a grumble to a scream as it hurtles out of the tunnel.

We want to know. But we can't know, really. Not with any certainty. Not until it comes for each of us. But we want to know. So, the following is what professionals tell us about what to expect when we get to the end.

Preparing for Approaching Death[1]

As a person enters the final stage of the dying process, two different dynamics are at work, closely interdependent. On the physical plane, the body begins the final process of shutting down, which will end when all physical systems cease to function. Usually this is orderly and unromantic, a progressive series of physical changes that are not medical emergencies requiring invasive interventions. These physical changes are a normal, natural way in which the body prepares itself to stop, and the most appropriate kinds of responses are comfort-enhancing measures.

Another dynamic of the dying process at work is on the emotional, spiritual, and mental plane; this is a different kind of process. The spirit of the dying person begins the final release from the body, from its immediate environment, and from all attachments. This release tends to follow its own priorities, which may include the resolution of whatever is unfinished of a practical nature and reception of permission to "let go" from family members. These events are the normal, natural way in which the spirit prepares to move from this existence into the next dimension of life. The most appropriate kinds of responses to the emotional, spiritual, and mental changes are those that support and encourage this release and transition.

---

[1] This section, Copyright © North Central Florida Hospice, Inc., 1996. This article was made publicly available in the hope that it will benefit others in the hospice community.

When a person's body is ready and wants to shut down, but the person is still unresolved over some important issue or with some significant relationship, he or she may tend to linger to finish whatever needs finishing despite discomfort or debilitation. Alternatively, when a person is emotionally, spiritually, and mentally resolved and ready for this release, but his or her body has not completed its final physical shutdown, the person will continue to live until that shutdown process is complete.

The experience we call death occurs when the body completes its natural process of shutting down, and when the spirit completes its natural process of reconciling and finishing. These two processes need to happen in a way that is appropriate and unique to the values, beliefs, and lifestyle of the dying person. Therefore, as you seek to prepare yourself for this event, the members of your hospice care team want you to know what to expect and how to respond in ways that will help your loved one accomplish this transition with support, understanding, and ease. You have the opportunity to provide this great gift as your loved one approaches this moment.

The emotional, spiritual, mental, and physical signs and symptoms of impending death that follow are offered to help you understand the natural kinds of things that may happen and how you can respond appropriately. Not all of these signs and symptoms will occur with every person, nor will they occur in this particular sequence. Each person is unique and needs to do things in his or her own way. This is not the time to try to change your loved one, but rather the time to give full acceptance, support, and comfort.

Normal Physical Signs and Symptoms
of Approaching Death

Coolness: The person's hands and arms, feet, and then legs may be increasingly cool to the touch: at the same time, the color of the skin may change. This is a normal indication that the circulation of blood is decreasing to the body's extremities and being reserved for the most vital organs. Keep the person warm with a blanket (not electric).

Sleeping: The person may spend an increasing amount of time sleeping, and may appear to be uncommunicative or unresponsive and at times may be difficult to rouse. This normal change is due in part to changes in the metabolism of the body. Sit with your loved one, hold his or her hand, but do not shake it or speak loudly. Speak softly and naturally. Plan to spend time with your loved one during those times when he or she seems most alert or awake. Do not talk about the person in the person's presence. Speak to him or her directly as you normally would, even though there may be no response. Never assume that the person cannot hear; hearing is the last of the senses to be lost.

Disorientation: The person may seem to be confused about the time, place, and identity of people surrounding him or her, including close and familiar people. This, too, is due in part to changes in metabolism. Identify yourself by name before you speak rather than asking the person to guess who you are. Speak softly, clearly, and truthfully when you need to communicate something important for the patient's comfort, such as, "It is time to take your medication," and offer an explanation, such as, "so you won't begin to hurt." Do not use this method to try to manipulate the patient to meet your needs.

Incontinence: The person may lose control of urine and/or bowel matter as the muscles in that area begin to relax. Discuss with your hospice nurse what can be done to protect the bed and to keep your loved one comfortable.

Normal Emotional, Spiritual, and Mental Signs and Symptoms

Withdrawal: The person may seem unresponsive, withdrawn, or in a comatose-like state. This indicates preparation for release, a detaching from surroundings and relationships, and the beginning of letting go. Since hearing remains all the way to the end, speak to your loved one in your normal tone of voice, identifying yourself by name when you speak, hold his or her hand, and say whatever you need to say that will help the person let go.

Vision-like experiences: The person may speak or claim to have spoken to others who have already died, or to see or have seen places not presently accessible or visible to you. This does not indicate a hallucination or a drug reaction. The person is beginning to detach from this life and is being prepared for the transition so that it will not be frightening. Do not contradict, explain away, belittle, or argue about what the person claims to have seen or heard. Just because you cannot see or hear it does not mean it is not real to your loved one. Affirm his or her experiences as normal and common.

Restlessness: The person may perform repetitive and restless tasks. This may in part indicate that something still unresolved or unfinished is disturbing him or her, and prevents him or her from letting go. Your hospice team members will assist you in identifying what may be happening and help you find ways to help the person find release from tension or fear. Other things that may be helpful in calming the person are to recall a place the person enjoyed, a favorite experience, read something comforting, play music, and give assurance that it is okay to let go.

Fluid and food intake decrease: When the person wants little or no fluid or food, this may indicate readiness for the final shutdown. Do not try to force food or fluid. You may help your loved one by giving permission to let go whenever he or she is ready. At the same time, affirm the person's ongoing value to you and the good you will carry forward into your life that you received from him or her.

Decreased socialization: The person may want to be with only a very few people or even just one person. This is a sign of preparation for release and affirms from whom the support is most needed to make the appropriate transition. If you are not part of this inner circle at the end, it does not mean you are not loved or are unimportant. It means you have already fulfilled your task with your loved one, and it is time for you to say goodbye. If you are part of the final inner circle of support, the person needs your affirmation, support, and permission.

Unusual communication: The person may make a seemingly out-of-character or non-sequitur statement, gesture, or request. This indicates that he or she is ready to say goodbye and is testing you to see if you are ready to let go. Accept the moment as a beautiful gift when it is offered. Kiss, hug, hold, cry, and say whatever you need to say to your loved one.

Giving permission and saying goodbye: Giving your loved one permission to let go, without making him or her feel guilty for leaving or trying to keep him or her with you to meet your own needs, can be difficult. A dying person will normally try to hold on, even though it brings prolonged discomfort, to be sure that those who are going to be left behind will be all right. Therefore, your ability to release the dying person from this concern and give him or her assurance that it is all right to let go whenever he or she is ready is one of the greatest gifts you have to give your loved one at this time.

When the person is ready to die and you are able to let go, then is the time to say goodbye. Saying goodbye is your final gift of love to your loved one, for it achieves closure and makes the final release possible. It may be helpful to lie in bed and hold the person, or to take his or her hand and then say everything you need to say.

It may be as simple as saying, "I love you." It may include recounting favorite memories, places, and activities you shared. It may include saying, "I'm sorry for whatever I have contributed to any tension or difficulties in our relationship." It may also include saying, "Thank you."

Tears are a normal and natural part of saying goodbye. Tears do not need to be hidden from your loved one or apologized for. Tears express your love and help you let go.

How Will You Know When Death Has Occurred?

Although you may be prepared for the death process, you may not be prepared for the actual moment of death. It may be helpful for you and your family to think about and discuss what you would do if you were the one present at the moment of death. The death of a hospice patient is not an emergency. Nothing must be done immediately.

The signs of death include such things as no breathing, no heartbeat, release of bowel and bladder, no response, eyelids slightly open, pupils enlarged, eyes fixed on a certain spot, no blinking, jaw relaxed and mouth slightly open. A hospice nurse will come to assist you if needed or desired. If not, phone support is available.

The body does not have to be moved until you are ready. Call the funeral home when you are ready to have the body moved, and identify the person as a hospice patient. The police do not need to be called. The hospice nurse will notify the physician.

What Hospice Looks Like

Myths, History, a Vision, a Calling

The World Waits

The world waits patiently to pass through the black
Curtain into a brightly lighted room
The gray white world is filled with anticipation
Night sounds echo as in a silent tomb
There is no present now, only the expectation
Of a gold and silver shimmering time
The earth waits, suspended, held breathless
Listening for the claxon chime
Of life when blood will flow warmly through
All living things and
God waves his hand and bids us love
And sends us spring again.

-        Jack Moore

Myths

Two weeks. By the time a family signs on to hospice, they have an average of two weeks left with their loved one. But hospice care is available to anyone who has a life-limiting illness. A person may be entitled to as much as six months of specialized care. If they require continued care beyond six months, they can have more. Sadly, most people come late to the party and they miss out on receiving the education and quality of attention at the end of life that are available to them. Why is that? Most likely, they don't understand it.

When my friend told me his mother had been diagnosed with stage IV lung cancer, he added, "There isn't much they can do for her now."

Naturally, I asked, "Is she in hospice?"

"No," he replied. "She's at home. My dad is caring for her."

By his response, I knew he either hadn't heard about hospice care or didn't understand it.

Not uncommonly, my friend's introduction to the concept of hospice care would be a very personal one. Advocates are working tirelessly to get the word out, but until they reach everyone, myths and misunderstandings will persist. Following are some of the most common myths about hospice.

Myth #1
People think hospice is a place.

This is likely due to the way the word *hospice* is used. I had asked, "Is your mother in hospice?" rather than, "Is your mother receiving hospice care?"

The word hospice derives from the word hospitality, which is what hospice is: a series of kindnesses, a system of helping people—patients and their families—to find comfort during a difficult journey.

Many cities do have hospice-oriented centers where people can live out their final days, but hospice still refers to activities rather than buildings. Hospice centers have a home-like atmosphere; some are actually converted single-family houses. In this setting, families of terminally ill people share kitchen and conversation space with other families. Patients have private bedrooms and, in keeping with the spirit of hospice, primary care is provided by loved ones whenever possible. These centers are not the norm for hospice care. Although trends vary by region and country, many people remain in their own residence while receiving hospice care; that residence could be a private home, nursing home, or residential facility.

When our dad was diagnosed with terminal cancer, he and our mother were residents in an assisted-living facility. They were able to combine the education and services that the hospice organization provided with the services they were already receiving through their assisted-living contract.

According to the National Hospice and Palliative Care Organization, in 2011, more than 66 percent of hospice patients were in their own residence at the time of death. Around 26 percent died in a designated Hospice Inpatient

Facility, and only about 7 percent died in an Acute Care Hospital.

Dad's death was the first hospice experience at River Village, the assisted-living facility where he lived at the time of his diagnosis. Most residents of that facility, we were told, went to a hospital when death was imminent. After our indoctrination, this changed. The management there hadn't realized that hospice is not a place. Home is a place, and hospice—hospitality—can happen there, wherever home happens to be.

Myth #2

People think hospice is a death sentence.

It is a goal of hospice care to help people understand that there is never "nothing more that can be done." Hospice care is a form of treatment; it is recommended when a cure is no longer a possibility, and so it becomes a part of the process of dying. However, many people find relief when harsh therapies end and palliative or comfort care begins, and they may live longer than expected.

It's okay for a person to change his or her mind. If a patient starts hospice care and either improves (it happens) or decides to resume life-saving treatments (yes, it happens), he or she can disengage from hospice care and come back to it later on. A life won't be lengthened or shortened due to hospice care, but quality of life is almost always improved.

Myth #3

People think hospice is expensive.

In the United States, support for end-of-life care has become a standard, and can be paid for through Medicare, Medicaid, and by most private insurance companies. Many hospices will provide care regardless of a patient's ability to pay.

According to the National Hospice and Palliative Care Organization, "The Medicare hospice benefit, enacted by Congress in 1982, is the predominate source of payment for hospice care." In 2011, 84 percent of hospice patients were covered by the Medicare hospice benefit versus other payment sources for the majority of their hospice experience.

Often, services a patient was paying for out of pocket, such as bathing and respite for caregivers, will be covered once hospice care begins, relieving families of these financial burdens.

Myth #4

People think they have to wait for a doctor to bring it up.

It's okay to say the H word. Doctors spend years in medical school learning how to save lives. End-of-life care is not at the top of most doctors' agendas, thankfully. Therefore, they may not be quick to shout out the "H" word during care planning discussions. Our family knew about hospice, but we were hesitant to bring it up before the doctor did. This man who was our father had no life limit. He was not planning to die. Ever.

We were not new to death; we had seen it before. Friends, family... even our teenaged brother had forged ahead. We lived in a place where so many people died of cancer every year that tests were conducted and the city's water wells were demolished and rebuilt; yes, there was something in the water. Yet the law of averages (for example, on average, 100 percent of people die during their lifetimes), didn't apply to us.

We were grateful when Dad's internist offered a referral. If yours does not, then it's okay to ask. Asking about it will prompt the doctor to explain how and when hospice might fit into the care plan.

Myth #5
People think hospice means relinquishing control.

When faced with terminal illness, sometimes people resist passing care-giving responsibilities on to strangers. No worries there. During hospice, professionals are available to support and instruct, but the family is in charge.

So, What Is Hospice Really Like?

Have you ever walked into a hospital or nursing home and immediately noticed the odor of sickness in the air? Hospice has a different smell. Hospice smells like sleeplessness and memories and hot dish and candles and Lysol and a window open. And it smells like clean sheets, picnics on the patio, and fresh flowers. Its sounds are not from monitors or machines; its sounds are quiet conversations, rock concerts, meditation, laughter. Hospice has the feel of people helping each other.

Hospice takes all comers. Everyone is qualified to be a warden in the prison of dying. Anyone can be a gardener in the conservatory of death. All voices are invited to sing in its choir.

Hospice isn't complicated. I attended a party once where I knew no one. It was a back-to-school event for parents, meant to be an icebreaker among strangers sharing the common bond of high tuition bills and decent prospects for the future success of our darlings. According to the instructions in an e-mail, I had dutifully toted along a tray of appetizers to share. Hummus, probably, and pita bread. Cheap, easy, universally acceptable. I rang the bell and the door was answered by a lovely teenager who greeted me warmly, told me her name, and removed the tray from my hands.

"The guests are in the living room. I'll set this on the buffet for you," she said, still smiling. "Does your dish require any preparation?" Gracefully, she helped a stranger feel at ease. She met me in my nervous place and simply led me in the right direction.

Likewise, during our dad's hospice, my sister Mickey was early on in her first conversation with our assigned hospice nurse when the tears began to fall.

"I'm sorry," Mickey said. "I know we're just having a conversation. I don't know why I'm crying now."

The nurse took Mickey's face between her hands and planted a big smooch on her forehead.

"I know," the nurse told Mickey. "I know."

"Was that a little creepy?" someone asked Mickey later.

"It was such a comfort," she explained. "That nurse had known me all of fifteen minutes, and she knew exactly what I needed."

This exchange is not unusual. Not that hospice providers go around kissing each other's foreheads, but that they help one another to find the way through this emotionally charged event. Hospice isn't so much about sickness; it's more about people helping each other. Hospitality.

Hospice: A Quick History

Dying with Hope, Dignity, and Love

My father's strength has left his arms
His legs bend beneath his weightlessness
His people feel his charms
His loving words, his gratefulness
Grace emanates and casts a light
Leaving only his Soul and his Spirit with us

-        Lindy

Hospice has evolved along a one-directional trajectory, gaining acceptance according to growing awareness of the concept. If death began somewhere around the book of Genesis (you are made of dust and unto dust you shall return), then comfort care followed just a few pages behind:

> The Lord is close to the brokenhearted and saves those who are crushed in spirit. (Psalm 34:18)

As the idea of caring for the dying became recognized across France, England, and Ireland in the 1800s, the word hospice became attached to it. Hospice as a concept moved into the mainstream in the late 1960s when Dame Cicely Saunders started St. Christopher's Hospice.

As the story goes, she and a patient had discussed that there might be a place that was better suited to pain control and preparing for death than a busy hospital ward. When he died, the patient bequeathed £500 to Saunders and told her to make something happen. He said, "I will be a window in your home." Since then, their ideals have migrated around the world.

Another push came in 1969 when the book titled *On Death and Dying* was published, sharing with the world the insights of Dr. Elisabeth Kübler -Ross, who wrote about her interviews with hundreds of dying patients. Kübler-Ross' experience led her to believe that home-based care was preferable over institutional care, and insisted that patients should be able to participate in decisions regarding their own treatment.

An Inspired Vision

Our family friends, the Willettes, were instrumental in bringing hospice to southern Minnesota. According to Gail Wenner, writing for *Circles of Care*, a newsletter published by Renville County Hospital, this family's voyage into hospice had a lasting impact on their community. Wenner describes the situation and the family:

> ...whose courageous spirit and creativity ushered in the concept of hospice care to our area in 1984. In the mid-1980s, most deaths in the Renville County area occurred in the hospital following aggressive curative treatment. The concept of hospice was new in the United States and not well-known or understood.
>
> Upon learning of her prognosis of terminal cancer, Lois Willette made the decision to live out her final days at home with the help of her large family and many friends. She knew instinctively the immense value of family involvement and community support during this difficult time. Friends were

not surprised at her bold determination to go against the established "rules" of the day. They describe her, with a smile, as an energetic woman of wit and wisdom who had a unique style, an artistic flair, and an amazing capacity for getting things done—especially those things that would benefit her family and her faith community.

Lois and [her husband] DePaul didn't know at the time that their coordination of Lois' care at home would trigger an enormous interest in hospice which eventually motivated a group of volunteers to establish Renville County Hospice from the ground up. After Lois' death, DePaul became a Hospice Board member and gave generously of his time, wisdom and pro bono legal assistance.

Renville County Hospice staff, team, patients, families, and volunteers express heartfelt gratitude to the Willette family for their inspired vision of bringing to our dying loved ones hope, dignity and love.

A Calling

Meanwhile, our family's personal journey with hospice was well under way. Describing the day he left for the army in 1943, Dad drew a lovely picture of his grandmother:

My grandma is tiny and frail, but love and compassion give her strength. She is the person called when a neighbor falls ill, or in the Irish tradition, to hold the head of the sick and dying. When there is a death in the neighborhood, the bereaved family often invites my Grandma Julia to sit with them through the night in a candlelit room where the body rests.

Years later, unaware of Great-Grandma Julia's story, I felt the complicated urge to do the same thing. Not as simple as a neighbor's knock on the back door: by the twenty-first century, hospice volunteer work involved an online application, a telephone screening, reference checks, in-person interviews, immunizations, certifications, and ongoing training.

During my interview, a hospice coordinator asked, "Why do you want to do this?"

I was embarrassed, but I had come this far, so I told her the truth, "I don't know."

The coordinator grinned and replied, "You'd be surprised by how many people say that."

Good Medicine

Directives, Pharmaceuticals, Pets & Healing Touch

Health Care Directives

Perfectly healthy people don't think about What If. They do not imagine their in-laws arguing with their children regarding the yes or no of a cord running over to the wall or a tube crawling down a throat. Perfectly healthy people don't think about dying, or almost dying, or dying and coming back to life. Perfectly healthy people are too busy living to consider the pros and cons of passing a perfectly good kidney to someone who just might need it more than they do. Perfectly healthy people don't have time for planning funerals: theirs or anyone else's.

So who, exactly, are all those people lined up for chemotherapy and dialysis and stretched out on gurneys in the emergency rooms of hospitals all over the country? Who goes to their neighborhood clinic with a painless lump or a mole or a sore that won't heal? Perfectly healthy people, that's who.

Not to scare anybody, but this Thanksgiving, take a look around the holiday table. Consider that these are precisely the people, your next of kin, who will likely be called upon to make decisions regarding your end-of-life care, your extended vegetative state, and possibly even your hygiene when Alzheimer's or another debilitating illness leaves you incapable of managing on your own. These folks who are spilling coffee and battling for the drumsticks are the same folks who will be sobbing around your bedside, yes. But are you sure the decisions they make will be the decisions you would make for yourself if you could? Would you wish upon them the guilt of pulling a plug and then wondering if that was, in fact, the death you would have wanted?

A Health Care Directive allows you to choose and name a specific person who will make health care decisions on your behalf when you are unable to make those decisions for yourself. The directive states, in writing, what your preferences are regarding nutrition, life support, organ donation, and more.

A Health Care Directive can encompass a variety of end-of-life solutions including a Living Will, Medical Power of Attorney, and DNR/DNI Documents:

Living Will: Legal document stating the types of medical treatment and life-sustaining measures that you want or do not want. Employment of artificial breathing and nutrition administered through a tube are some possibilities to consider.

Medical Power of Attorney: Legal document naming the person who will make medical decisions on your behalf.

DNR/DNI AND Allow a Natural Death:

- DNR (**Do Not Resuscitate**) is a request to not have CPR (Cardiopulmonary Resuscitation) if your heart stops or your breathing ceases.
- DNI (**Do Not Intubate**) is a request that allows for chest compressions or cardiac medications to be used, but a breathing tube will not be inserted.
- Adding, "**AND Allow a Natural Death**" directs caregivers that no steps should be taken that will interfere with a natural death; excellent care will be provided for the sake of comfort and leading to a calm and peaceful death, but

these words indicate that the patient wishes to avoid treatments such as artificial feedings, fluids, and other measures that will prolong the process of dying without adding to quality of life.

All of these orders are reversible and can be withdrawn at any time by the patient or by the person who holds power of attorney for the patient. As long as the patient is able to participate in these decisions, the DNI/DNR discussion should continue. Likewise, when a person has made a firm decision in this regard, it is the responsibility of caregivers to honor the patient's wishes, even if those wishes conflict with the desires of the people around him or her.

Whether your decision is to resuscitate or not, this specific information should be posted where a paramedic entering your home can easily see it.

The day before Dad died, after ten of us had camped out in his apartment for most of the previous seven days and nights, I noticed, taped to a cupboard above the stove, two prominent sheets of canary yellow paper. These sheets were identical except for the names written at the top of each one. The sheet with my mother's name at the top indicated she is to be resuscitated. The sheet with my father's name at the top said the same thing.

These twin documents were posted the day my parents moved into their apartment. Like kids' drawings on the fridge, the screaming neon reminders had been hanging there for so long that none of us saw them anymore. However, a paramedic called to the scene would search for them, would easily find them, and would be obligated to follow their instructions.

The day they were taped to the cupboard, they were accurate. Yes, save our healthy parents from an untimely death. But over the past month, things had changed dramatically for our father. We were in a different mode now; we had a different understanding. As much as I wished for my dad to live, the prospect of him being aggressively resuscitated at this point seemed unthinkable, even cruel.

Sharon was nearby, humming to herself while scooping orange sherbet into bowls for Mom and Dad. I tapped her on the shoulder and pointed at the screaming yellow sign.

She looked at it closely, and then jumped back as if I'd shown her a life-sized poster of those two little girls in that hallway in *The Shining*.

"Throw it out!" she demanded, looking away. I couldn't. As a hospice volunteer, if I had seen the same document, I would have asked the patient or his family or a hospice nurse whether the form should be updated.

At this stage in the game, for us, it seemed almost too late for updates. And too near the end to throw away anything that was at one time meant to keep my father alive. These are irrational thoughts, and not uncommon. People do the strangest things when they are grieving. People move bright yellow sheets of paper to the insides of cupboards, hidden away but not gone altogether. Just in case. In case? In case the world suddenly reverses its spin, moving backward on its axis, erasing time until my father returned to his not-yet-dying condition?

Never mind what I did. What you'll do is remember to help a loved one update his directive as the situation warrants.

Organ Donation: Reduce, reuse, and recycle, right? You already know you can't take it with you. But you might be able to help someone else. Specify in your Health Care Directive what your preferences are regarding eye and tissue donation. Did you know? The list of your body's parts eligible for recycling is long and growing along with medical advancements. What you choose to donate may be limited by your cause of death, but plan for an ideal scenario, where everything you are willing to part with can be put to good use after you have moved away from your physical body, if your religious and personal beliefs allow.

My friend elected to donate his entire body for scientific study. If this is your desire, contact the medical school nearest your home for guidance.

Free Health Care Directive forms and information are available online in abundance—you can't help but trip over them—and they are quick and easy to complete. Do everybody a favor and make this happen.

Once you have named a decision maker, ensure that the person knows he or she is the chosen one and is okay with that. Further, give copies of your Directive to a few people to hold onto. A Health Care Directive locked in a safe deposit box is worthless, unless you are planning to unlock it before you crash your motorcycle or meet some other calamity. Gruesome, yes, but stuff happens. It happens to perfectly healthy individuals.

Block off a Saturday morning and get this task out of the way. Perhaps, if you have a Health Care Directive, you will never need one. Perhaps, if you don't, you might.

Pharmaceuticals

Comparing notes following the death of his mother, my friend told me, "My family had a different experience than yours regarding medication. Before we had hospice help, we made managing medication way more difficult than it had to be. Having sisters fly in from out of town at different times exacerbated the medication situation as each one would attempt to make it easier to track and administer."

He went on, "We 'in town' kids each had a different perspective because, when Mom was in and out of the hospital, we were there at different times; each nurse or doctor gave what seemed to be conflicting instructions and different medications that they wanted Mom to try. My dad couldn't keep it all straight and didn't ask questions. It was a mess and we wasted a lot of time and energy trying to sort it out.

"That's where hospice was so helpful. Not that they took it over, but they were a calm, encouraging force. They reassured us that we weren't going to make mistakes and reminded us about what hospice was for: comfort and quality of life."

Hospice doctors, pharmacists, and nurses will provide careful guidance regarding the medications prescribed for use during hospice. One of many ongoing discussions, medication management is an important part of the hospice agenda among all of these team members.

At Dad's Hospice Intake Meeting, we were told that a Care Kit would be brought to River Village containing a variety of medications meant to treat pain and nausea. I was raised in the olden days, when the medicine du jour was most likely to be a Popsicle and St. Joseph's Aspirin for Children.

My grandmother advocated for a spoonful of brandy over prescription medications for most aches and pains. Being the ride-it-out types, it was important for my family members, as caregivers, to understand that hospice is a different kind of situation. During hospice, quick, appropriate comfort is the goal. "Riding it out" is not.

Start appropriate medications early, rather than holding off until pain is excruciating. When it was time to start helping Dad with medication, the group present had no question in their minds. They could read the pain on his face. Their strongest instinct and most pressing need were to "help him."

Are you looking for a chart listing hospice-related medications, along with their standard dosage requirements? Sorry, can't help you there. The people who know those specifics are trained medical professionals, and even they will tell you that, once the medicating is under way, there can be a system, but there is no usual dose. Some people need very little medication, whereas others need much larger doses to achieve the same effect.

What about chemical dependency? When you think about it, you realize that drug addiction is not a concern when a person is very near to death. Hospice-trained doctors and nurses will provide guidance on administering the lowest necessary dose to keep the patient comfortable and still aware of his or her surroundings. They will also provide guidance on managing potential side effects.

Pets

If the world were suddenly split down its middle, with animal lovers on one hemisphere and not-animal-lovers on the other, I believe most people would easily find their place and, once there, would not attempt to cross over. I imagine animal-loving is a genetic thing: blue eyes or brown, straight hair or curly, animal person or not. Our family is divided that way. Either you own a pet store or you don't. For those on the pro-animal side of the equation, pets can play a magical role in comfort care.

Our friend Rose is one of those pro-animal types. When she drove up to Minnesota from Virginia to assist her mother in her last days, she brought the family dog along in the car, thinking she'd find someplace to board him in the city where she would be staying.

"Oh, no," said her mother. "The dog stays here."

And so he did. At the foot of her bed, following her to the living room or kitchen, later tucked in among the covers. It was true love and a real comfort to Rose's mother and to Rose. An unexpected gift.

Trained therapy dogs (and cats and rabbits) thrive on positively impacting the lives of people who are dying. Beyond ordinary obedience instruction, these dogs and their owners go through extensive training programs specific to therapy work. During training, they and their human partners are subjected to the many surprises they will encounter when visiting sick people in homes or care centers, including wheelchairs, walkers, canes, loud voices, strange smells, sudden movements, and squealing machines.

What do therapy animals and Justin Bieber have in common? They both get mobbed when they enter a building. Observing therapy animals at work, it seems that everyone wants to pet them; everyone has a story to tell. Patients who are reluctant to speak, are depressed, or are experiencing physical pain may turn inward. When a trained dog comes along, these people often feel more comfortable opening up.

Alice was a ninety-two-year-old patient who had been around dogs throughout her life. When I met her, she was passing her last days in a nursing home, mostly silently. A therapy dog approached and sat quietly beside Alice's wheelchair; in response, she instinctively stroked the dog and said, "Good boy." This was a watershed moment for Alice's family and friends. To the dog, however, this was just another day on the job.

Palliative care is about comfort. If your person has been an animal lover in the past, be open to this kind of experience now. Don't go buy anyone a parakeet or anything, but if your hospice organization offers pet therapy (many do) you might want to give it a try.

Healing Touch

Ouch! Skinned knee? Here's a Band-Aid. All better! Fired? Unfriended? Dumped? How about a hug?

Like every other aspect of the good life, death has its raw and uncomfortable moments. Hospice teams will guide patients through the maze of medications that can alleviate discomfort, but understand that medication is only one piece of the comfort puzzle. The same hospice professionals will also be able to guide you through the amazing world of healing. Not curing; that is something else. But healing: relieving suffering either without or in tandem with prescribed medications.

Many hospice volunteers receive supplemental training in hand massage and healing touch, skills they readily pass along to family caregivers. Hospice is about hospitality, but it is also about teaching. Hospice associates are trained to teach and to empower families themselves to provide the care that will keep their loved one comfortable.

Because healing is in our nature as humans, learning simple ways to share appropriate, gentle touch to soothe someone comes easily. Start here: take your person's hand. See, that wasn't so hard. Sit quietly. Your grasp should be firm; tighten it up until you feel the press of his or her hand against your own. Mean it when you touch someone. Rather than a tickle, you are going for a true connection. A gentle connection, but an authentic one.

Remember always to watch and listen, even if your loved one is asleep or unable to speak. A furrowed brow or wincing indicates pain, which means Stop. If your touch is welcome, you might see the person relax physically; clenched fists will fall open and shoulders will loosen up. Ask, "Is this okay?" and stop when your touch is no longer helping. Following are some simple ways to heal and soothe a favorite person.

Sweet Cheeks: My friend John went through an entire job interview with boundless enthusiasm. At the end of the interview, he asked the manager if there was anything else he needed to know.

"Yes," said the manager. "I need to know when you're going to zip up your zipper." John's cheeks immediately burned crimson. He quickly zipped up. And he did get hired, by the way.

People tend to blush when facing embarrassment, shame, or regret; cheeks store the memories of these feelings. To comfort someone in a gentle way, and to relieve them of these memories, use the back of your hand and the backs of your fingers to stroke the cheek upward and away toward the temple once or twice.

Dad responded to this touch by turning his cheek toward me. When I repeated the movement, he smiled. Don't assume that if your person melts under the stroke of his cheek, that he has much to be ashamed of. A long life brings its unzipped moments, and a short life does, too. Contented, healthy infants also appreciate this gesture.

Soothe the Spine: If your loved one is spending time on his back or side, stroking the spine can relieve and sedate him. Start at the nape of the neck and with your hand open, use your palm to sweep downward to the tailbone. This is one long, slow, easy movement. Pause and repeat, top of spine to tailbone.

Rockabye: Some people find comfort in rocking, even pulling into a fetal position at times. This is soothing; think of a small child rocking in a cradle or someone snoozing in a hammock at the lake. What's more relaxing than that?

Pucker Up: A kiss is well known for its curative properties. A kiss to the lips or forehead will be welcome, according to your relationship. Not in a weird way, but in the way you always have done it. Kissing my dad on the forehead relaxed his entire body. When Mom kissed his lips, he said, "I love that!" Keep the lips moist with swabs and with lip balm. Swab the mouth and tongue frequently to remove the natural gunk that collects there. Are you squeamish? Do it anyway, or ask someone to help you out. Your loved one likely would do as much for you.

Free the Feet: Feet are a powerful part of the body. Feet take you there. Feet take a beating all through life, and yet contain nerve connections to every other part of the body. Many people who care for the dying want to keep the feet covered. A person gets restless and kicks the covers off his feet; the caregiver tucks the covers tightly around and under the mattress so he can't do that anymore. But what you need to know about this is that a dying person frequently wants their feet to be free. Instead of tucking them in, pull the covers back away from the feet, keeping the rest of the person's body covered. When the feet are released, a person often relaxes visibly. You can't go wrong by freeing the feet.

It's okay to hold on to your person's feet, too, either tightly around the arch of the foot, or stretching your hand over the tops of the ankles; place your thumb on one side of the foot and the rest of your hand on the other, so the webbed part of your hand between your thumb and everything else is like a bridge, connecting one ankle to the other. Now press the web of your hand onto the top of the foot. Watch your person's face and let all that good energy pass between you. When you comfort someone, by the way, you feel better too.

The Sound of Music: Music brings peace and calm to most people at the end of life. Here's the thing, though. Don't think that spiritual hymns or classical music are the only options. Whether a family likes it or not, the guy who grew up blasting Led Zeppelin is going to prefer rock over opera any day, even in his dying days. The best, most comforting music is the stuff he has always enjoyed. Smooth jazz was huge in our dad's life, and so in his death. We tried to guess what he might like to hear, and ultimately settled on whatever Mom selected, agreeing that, as usual, Mother probably knew best.

Motion Is Lotion: Ahh, the heavenly sensation of just getting comfortable, snuggling under a blanket, plumping the pillows just right, finally relaxed and… was that the doorbell? Moving a person who is dying, once they're finally content, feels like tough love. It is and it isn't. Every couple of hours, a person needs to be moved. Just a little. Nurse Cathy busted us on this.

"Remember to move him from his back to his side," she said gently.

"It seems to hurt him when we move him," we replied, fully willing to break any rules that didn't seem to apply to our situation.

"When the skin is so thin, we want to avoid pressure sores by shifting positions," she said gently.

"Yes, but he's only been in bed since this morning," we argued. Some of us are lawyers; we can't help ourselves.

"Two hours," she said gently. "Bed sores can start in a short time. Especially here, under his feet." Dad was on his back and she tenderly lifted one foot to show us the backs of his heels, just beginning to look pink, the skin tearing slightly. "Every two hours," she continued, ever so gently. "You can change his position just after giving him medication; he'll be more comfortable then. Move him from his back to his side, from his side to his back, and then to the other side. Use the pillows to support his arms and his back. A towel or sheet between his knees will keep them from rubbing together."

Okay, okay.

When we moved Dad, his view changed. We paid attention to his reactions and noticed he showed interest in his mother's photo on a desk across the room. Someone took it to him. He held the photo with both hands, lifted it up, and then brought it close to his face. He kissed the picture and oh, what a smile.

Beds, Baths, and Golf Shirts

It is possible to bathe a person in a bed. It is possible to change someone's clothes without asking him to sit up. It is even possible to change the bedsheets while a person is wrapped in them, asleep. No, these are not dorm-room pranks. These are useful nursing skills that anybody can learn. And there's nothing like clean sheets and a clean shirt when you've been sacked out in bed for a couple of days.

The trick with the bath is to put a plastic-lined pad under your person, so they don't have to lie on a wet mattress later on. The trick with the clothing is to cut a slit up the back of the shirt; this way, the clothes can easily go over the arms and head, but they don't get bunched up behind the back. The trick with changing the sheets is to have two people do this: one person who knows what he is doing, and one person who is willing to learn.

Dad's life in bed went on for a while. When he was ready for a clean shirt because we had spilled medicine on one or because the priest was coming back, we fixed up a new one. An aide helping out gasped a little when he noticed me sitting on the end of the bed wielding scissors.

"Did I do something wrong?" I asked.

"That's a pretty nice shirt," he said.

"I know. He likes the red ones," I answered.

Realizing he was still staring, I added, "He can't take it with him."

"Right, but..."

"Do you want it?" I was being sincere. "We have plenty. There's a whole closet full of golf shirts. He collects them, don't you, Dad?"

The aide stammered, "No, no, I just..." Then, a little red in the cheeks, he pulled on a pair of latex-free gloves and reached into his bucket of clear, warm water. He lifted a white washcloth from the water and began to sponge Dad's shoulders and back.

He was tender with Dad, as if Dad belonged to him, too. I really wanted to give him a whole pile of shirts, to repay him for his kindness. But health aides and volunteers cannot accept gifts, and the moment quietly slipped away.

After Dad died, someone offered to do the laundry for Mom. As I put Mom's clothes away in a drawer, I came across one of Dad's shirts, a bright yellow golf shirt with the Brightwood Hills logo on the front and a vertical slit cut up the middle of the back, stopping just below the collar. The tears came before I could stop them. It happens that way sometimes.

Bless Us, Oh, Lord

The world is round and a messy mortal is my friend.
Come walk with me in the mud.

-     Hugh Prather

Whatever you think about Heaven—that there is one, that there isn't one, that perhaps you have to hang out in a crowded little village called Purgatory or Limbo until your friends, through the jangling of their plastic beads, bail you out—let's agree for the moment that it is true. You can't prove it, I can't prove it, but let's just say it's a thing.

Now, take a good long look at your loved one. Think about his or her vision of the afterlife, or lack thereof. Your dying loved one is a lot closer to knowing the truth than the rest of the crowd gathered at his bedside, so let's agree, for the moment, that that person's vision, also, is true. Whether it coincides with yours or not, let's just say it's a thing.

Death stretches people. Death and dying test the faithful and agnostics alike, and, with mission critical in mind, well-meaning folks tend to muck things up when it comes to discussing death with the dying. People who wish to help will offer memorial Masses to people who have never been to Mass, prayers for people who prefer not to pray, and splashes of holy water to people who wish not to be splashed upon at this time, thank you very much. If this happens during your family's hospice journey, consider that as much as your universe is focused on you, your family, and most of all, your loved one, perhaps these offensive gestures are not really about y'all. Maybe praying for you helps them.

If exercising religious rituals in your family's name brings peace to some other household, if it bonds parents to children and classmates to teachers and friends to friends, does it honestly cause harm to you and yours? Seriously. Kind thoughts traveling in your loved one's direction? Look out! It's a good vibe! Ouch! I felt that one! Man, that chant's gonna hurt in the morning! Oh, wait. No, it won't.

On the other hand, please, generously hold your tongue if your faith is in conflict with your person's activities. Certain religious groups believe they are required to convert troubled souls. Word of advice? Don't save souls. Not now. You have no idea what lies in the heart of this person, so close to closing life's door behind him. Would you trouble him more by raising questions? Do you imagine that thoughts of an afterlife haven't crossed his mind?

As spiritual as our family always was, people along our paths felt compelled to save our apparently raggedy souls. Did they realize? We were as good as it gets. Mom and Dad spent nearly every morning of our teen years attending daily worship. They often had to shovel snow, move two cars, and drop a kid off at school to get there, but they went. Did the evangelists know? We said Grace before meals. We attended Catholic schools, Protestant vacation Bible school, and Covenant summer camp. We partied at friends' Bat Mitzvahs and Bar Mitzvahs. On rainy days we played Goodability, our grass-roots version of Sunday school, in the basement, led by the most Reverend Mickey Moore. We played church, using the stairs as our pews, and borrowed hymnals from St. J's to guide our services. Granted, playing church was more about eating chips and drinking grape juice before dinner than about anything religious, but it was part of us.

Through their living example, our parents passed along a few nuggets of wisdom regarding morality and good character, including the following:

- People are honest. If the kid says he shot a five on Hole Number 8, he shot a five.
- People deserve respect. Everyone has the same right to play golf, regardless of skin color; to work in sales, regardless of gender; to a decent education, regardless of the level of disdain expressed by the nun in a certain fifth-grade classroom; and to be treated decently, regardless of marital status.
- Only God knows what is in any person's heart. There's that proverb about who should throw the first stone, and it was retold regularly in our house, putting a nice finish on sibling squabbling.

So, free yourself. If your loved one's paganism worries you; if the zealous neighbor will not leave you alone; if someone brings a jug of magic water… and if someone else drinks it; if people let the chaplain in too often, or forget to call the rabbi altogether… free yourself. When death is in the room, lay your conversion burden at God's feet, if you believe there is a God and if you believe God has feet. A creator of the universe is too powerful to depend wholly on flawed human judgment regarding who makes the list at the night club in the afterworld. Let go of your human understanding. You have other things to attend to.

If you cannot let go, if you are still uncertain, think about it this way: Have you ever compared two snowflakes? Or studied the veins on a leaf? An architect of all natural things, including life itself, is way too creative to have designed a heavenly home with only one door. Even Macy's has a couple of entrances. Is it possible that Christians and Muslims and Jews and Buddhists are all right? Is it possible that oaks and maples thrive in the same forest? Do dolphins and whales share the seas? Does a candle become less bright for letting another candle share its flame?

Celebrating a Life
Services, Obituaries, Pallbearers, Parties

Memorial Service: Divide and Conquer

Every formal religious tradition has its own ideas about how a person should be honored after his or her death. Within the parameters of your own beliefs, you might be called upon to do some "planning" of memorial or funeral services. For those who carry no strict affiliation with one religious sect or another, only federal, state, and local ordinances will limit your creativity. Does your loved one wish to have his remains sent into the atmosphere on a firecracker? It has been done. Scattered into the sea? Set carefully on the mantel over the fireplace in the family cabin? Yes, these all have been done.

Whether you will honor your loved one in a traditional or more unique style, making decisions about how it will happen is a challenge no one should take on alone. Who should plan the service for your loved one? That's like asking who should sing tenor in the choir. Why, the person who sings tenor, of course. But a choir is made up of many voices. As is a funeral. Planning a funeral is best done by the person who is being laid to rest; but if that can't or hasn't happened, then it will become an exercise in Getting Along for the rabble. At least, it was for us. But we got through it.

Within a day or two of the intake meeting, a Listserv message went out with the subject line, "Mom is thinking about," and funeral planning was under way. Our collective bottom line was to be there for Mom, to do all we could do ourselves, while involving her as much or as little as she wished. We agreed that she and Dad would have the final say in all decisions, but we strived to contribute our time and talents to the extent that we could so that Mom could direct her energy toward Dad. Brian wrote:

> Mom is thinking about funeral planning, not in a morbid way, but because the social worker brought it up. I told her we would be on it, so she shouldn't have to worry about all of that now, no matter how long this journey is going to be.

At this stage, we had no real sense of how long this conversation could go on. Months? Weeks, at least, we thought. Better to get it out of the way, we thought. We were looking for things we could "do." This was something we could do. Mickey found a funeral planning guide and scheduled a conference call for all of us to discuss it. She wrote:

> The hospice people gave us some funeral planning materials. I think the best thing to do is look it over and divide and conquer.

Search the Internet or ask your hospice team or faith leaders for guidance on funeral or memorial service planning. Our pastor friend Father Bill provided a guidebook that included a wide selection of readings, songs, and prayers, as well as suggestions on creating literature to be used by attendees at the funeral service. He shared prayer cards and funeral booklets created by other families to give us some ideas. The tributes were colorful, and included photos, stories and poems. They seemed so private, and yet so helpful. It was a good place to start. We did take some liberties, with Father Bill's consent, and this made Dad's funeral memorable to us and impactful to others. More on that a little later.

One lengthy discussion point in our family was the eulogy. Who should have the pleasure of speaking out about the person Dad was and the life that he lived? Perhaps no one. Perhaps everyone. Or, perhaps, the deceased person himself.

Obituaries Are Expensive

Sharon: The obituary you wrote was nice, Terry, but do you think we should add that Dad was preceded in death by his parents?

Julie: At age 90, perhaps it is more notable if one is NOT preceded in death by one's parents?

Let's be practical. A typical obituary will cost something per line to publish. In some cities, publishing a death notice can feel like asking to be robbed. Yet, if you have the means, or if you can envision a way to stretch and find the means, you will be inclined to pay any price. Everyone must be told what a fabulous man this was! His contributions! His accomplishments! His full middle name!

Our first run at writing Dad's obituary resulted in an official notice longer than all of our right arms stretched end to end. The exercise made for animated conversation. We were effectively comparing notes on what each of us felt was critical information, and through that process, some of Dad's secret lives were exposed.

For example, one of the older kids wrote about Dad's contribution to the Evans Scholarship program. Although he'd never mentioned it to us, Mom confirmed that Dad had worked diligently to secure on-campus housing for Evans Scholars attending the University of Minnesota in the Twin Cities. She added, "He spent a lot of time in meetings then. He was gone an awful lot during that time."

Obit, Version One, was heavy on Dad's professional accomplishments but failed to mention his generosity; a scholarship fund he had founded, whose bylaws included language excluding his own children from eligibility, had by the time of his death awarded over $100,000 in grants to ambitious college students.

Clearly, the first draft was too long; not because we didn't want to share Dad with the newspaper-reading public. Rather, because Dad would not have wanted that. Although he bragged about his kids to the point of embarrassment, he was not the type to boast about himself. This fellow, who forged a career on the revenue of radio advertisements, was not inclined to spend money on self-promotion.

Here's a little secret: it is in life, not in death, that we impact other people. It is in life, not in death, that we have the opportunity to brag about one another, to boast about the incredible gift our loved one is to the world. It is in life, not in death, that we have the opportunity to say, "I'm sorry," and "I love you," and "Hey, Dad, you're pretty amazing." And, "I forgive you." And, "Thank you."

Our end result was an obituary that was decidedly brief. Ironically, several newspapers took up our baton and wrote their own accounts of Dad's life and contributions. This happened because of the way Dad had lived his life. He didn't need our help this time. He had a good story, and people out in the world thought it worth telling.

Why Pallbearers Are Usually Men

Mickey:	I suggest the pallbearers be the grandchildren who want to, oldest to youngest, boys and girls.
Funeral Director:	No.

If your ritual includes a casket, who should carry it? How to decide? Our funeral director might recommend an arm-wrestling competition, and with good reason. The duty of pallbearer should fall on the heartiest of the bunch. Pallbearer is a functional, not an honorary, role. Caskets are heavy. Pallbearers at funerals appear to have it easy as they wheel that beautiful box down the aisle of the sanctuary. Look a little closer. Do you detect a sense of the old advertisement, "Glad I used Dial," in those eyes?

The athletes who stand before you have hefted a solid wooden casket up two flights of stairs and have maneuvered the long, rectangular crucible around more than a few tight corners to deliver it to the gathering place. Later, they will convey said box back down several steps, heave it into a vehicle whose open door stands above waist height, and finally they will haul the thing up a snow-covered hill to its final resting place. All while carrying the additional weight of awareness that the body of a man they love rides inside.

Pallbearer service is an honor and a privilege. And a workout. The fact that pallbearers are usually able young men is not sexist; it is practical.

Parties

"I'm going to need some help here," Lindy's voice was calling us from the front hallway of the funeral home, her face hidden behind a stack of framed photographs hauled over from the apartment at River Village. As we stepped forward to help her, we saw her husband, Vern's, feet, behind her, his face hidden, too, behind boxes of plates, cups, napkins, forks, and spoons piled up in his arms. Things were shaping up to look more like a party than a funeral. And we were okay with that. We are Irish, after all.

Gathering together after a death can be comforting for the people left behind. Perhaps this is why so many different cultures and religious groups practice traditions that include some manner of gathering for survivors. Some congregate for an evening, others for seven days; others welcome visitors for thirteen days, and some for forty-nine intense days of mourning and remembrance.

Whether you decide to gather in a darkened bar for a wake, sit Shiva with family, or say a few words on a riverbank, this get-together should be planned with deep respect for the wishes of the deceased. What would your loved one feel is appropriate, according to his personal beliefs and traditions? What would this person appreciate?

People will say that a service or gathering provides "closure" for those left behind. I doubt relationships ever really "close." They transform and they live on—in our memories, our conversations, our guilt, and our gratitude.

Maybe people of various faiths agree on gathering together after a death because it is something they can do, something people before them have done, tradition.

Traditions provide guidelines; everyone appreciates a road map when traveling in new territory.

On what would have been Dad's ninetieth birthday, we waked: we laughed and basked in the great warmth we felt surrounded that winter night by old friends, neighbors, relatives, and all the others who had slipped in and out of Dad's life along the way, and were kind enough to celebrate that life with us. We shared a slideshow in a side room at the funeral home and we served, yes, birthday cake. Were we sad? We were heartbroken. But we were not lost. We were encircled and cared for. I think that's what the gathering is about.

Good Grief

A funny thing happened to a guy in my office. We almost had to let him go. Steve was forgetting everything. He forgot to check messages and forgot to return calls. He read e-mails and didn't respond. When he was asked for updates regarding work that should have been completed, Steve just shrugged and gave us a deer-in-the-headlights, what-am-I-doing-here stare. He seemed confused and the rest of the team was frustrated. One of his co-workers complained, "It's as if, on the day his mother died, Steve checked out." Aha! Steve was grieving—and not alone.

Workplace grief costs businesses more than $75 billion every year in reduced productivity, increased errors, and accidents. After a family member dies, sooner or later, people need to return to ordinary life. Some might even be eager to get back to work, with its routines and its paychecks. However, a well-documented phase of the grieving process, depression, can interfere with performance at work. In this stage of grief, the reality of a loss starts sinking in. A grieving person might experience difficulty sleeping, lack of appetite, low energy, and crying spells. The stresses of a normal day only compound the problem, so even a top employee may need some latitude and a few new tools to work through grief without letting his work go altogether.

Many companies have policies offering employees generous bereavement benefits. Knowing that a person has three days off with pay can ease his or her anxiety during an already difficult time. Usually, those three days are a blur, filled with planning, notifying people, and possibly traveling to a service. Those who have experienced losses of their own will understand: this is not a paid vacation.

When a person does return to work, he is unlikely to be "over it." Simply hearing, "I'm sorry for your loss," can help. He should say thank you, but should not expect colleagues to offer free counseling sessions. There is an elephant in the office; once it's been acknowledged, everyone needs to move on. If you are grieving and you need to talk, separate your work from your personal life as well as you can. Meet a close friend after work, or pay a professional. This is money well spent.

Forgetfulness is extremely common during grief, and may persist for several weeks. It usually presents as short-term memory loss; a simple conversation can become a snapchat, erased the minute it ends. Avoid frustration by putting expectations in writing. E-mail summaries and scheduled reminders are useful now. Piles of reminder notes might seem like overkill, but these prompts will help a person get through. Anyway, effective follow-up is a good habit; when this phase is over, which it will be, you can thank a deceased loved one for inadvertently improving your productivity at work.

Will life ever be normal again? Sure, of course. But it will be a different kind of normal. When a family friend, Mir, lost her husband, she wisely took advantage of every electronic tool available to keep herself together as her world fell apart, including reminders to ensure that mundane daily tasks occurred as they should: showers in the mornings, lunch at noon, trash to the curb on Thursdays. It helped. Months went by, and Mir knew she was moving toward a healthy new normal when she started cussing back at her computer. "If that thing tells me once more to go brush my teeth!"

Grieving people deserve to get the help that's needed when it is needed. Hand over your extra sticky-notes if you have to, if making stacks and stacks of notes seems to help a guy or gal get through the first few days and weeks after a loved one passes on. Loss lasts forever, but grief can eventually find itself a comfortable place in a corner of the heart, staying out of the way so everyone can move on with the business of living.

Reminders help. Hand over your sticky-notes
if someone you work with is grieving.

The Five Stages of Grieving[2]

They don't always happen in order, and just because you've made it through one round, that doesn't mean you won't have to face each stage again. Knowing about the normal stages of grief can help everyone travel through each stage more easily. When Mom seemed to be in the Anger phase, it was a great relief when my friend Mary put a name on it for me.

"She's kind of hard to live with today," I confided.

"Oh, she's in the ANGER stage! I remember when MY mom went through that. It was so out of character; we hardly recognized her. Don't worry. It doesn't last long."

---

[2] Introduced by Elisabeth Kübler-Ross in her book *On Death and Dying*, inspired by her many years of work with terminally ill people.

Grief

It's like a blanket falls over you
Unexpectedly, you are trapped alone in a primitive starless dark
Only With only the tranquil drum of the heart of the universe
To soothe you

Under the blanket,
Under humid scratchy black, is everything
Nothing outside it exists anymore
Not as it had, not as it will, now there is only now
And night and you trembling alone
Hoping the core of the universe might sustain you

It's like an ancient gray quilt drops its great weight over you
Time becomes slow time, heavy time, thick liquid time
Puddling under and around you where you wait
You catch your breath, you will each sigh to beat
In time with the colossal heart in your hands
You wish for fresh new air
Yet pray the next lungful arrives unchanged

It's like alternately kicking to get outside
And crouching frozen under the snow
Willing the day to play on this way forever

It's like a blanket is thrown over
And you underneath its weight wait alone
Your own thundering heart cradled in somnolent arms
You are scanning the darkness for stars

-            Julie

Part II

Something You Carry with You

Life Review

You should know, I am still Jack I. Moore.
I have not changed that much.

Wildflowers

Back in the days when pots and pans could speak, there lived a man. In order to have water, every day he had to walk down the hill and fill two pots and walk them home.

One day, it was discovered one of the pots had a crack and, as time went on, the crack widened. Finally, the pot turned to the man and said, "Every day you take me to the river and by the time you get home, half the water's leaked out. I am old and broken. Please replace me with a newer, better pot."

"Oh, no," said the man. "You don't understand. You see, as you spill, you water the wildflowers on the side of the path."

Indeed, along the side of the path where the pot was carried grew beautiful wildflowers, while the other side of the path was barren.

"I think I'll keep you," said the man.

- Traditional, shared by Kevin Kling

Dad's loving acceptance of his children was inversely proportionate to the amount it was tested, and this is what formed us. There were second and third chances to get things right, because he believed that, in the end, we were worth keeping. To call Dad an optimist is an understatement. He was, to his core, optimistic about all things: whether he'd find a #4 Titleist golf ball in the woods, whether the car would stop in a cornfield after the brakes went out, whether we kids would survive to adulthood. When my sister Mickey wrote her master's thesis on optimism, she used Dad as her subject.

Dad had faith that tomorrow would certainly be an improvement over today and this was something we could count on; even through adversity, his positivity never wavered. Thinking about it, our family dynamic has stayed pretty consistent over time. It is this way for many families.

Families are composed of people who knew you when: when you were awkward, when you were small, when you were frightened and trying to figure things out; they tend not to let you forget it. No matter how clean or cluttered a childhood, no matter whether one is raised to wrestle for scraps at dinner or passes youth gracefully grinning down from a pedestal, most humans escape their pasts eventually and forge paths uniquely their own. We did.

A person may become a business owner or special needs teacher, a Spanish translator, a stay-home parent, a Doctor of Law, Doctor of Chiropractic, Doctor of Orthopaedics, or Doctor of Gender in Renaissance Literature; we did. You may carve out a place in the adult world where you are powerful, confident, and competent; we did.

And then, like us, you will go home again, and the gate in your mind that protects your earliest memories and mannerisms swings open and you become, once again, the person your family knew you to be. It's as if our places are set at the table and a script is placed in front of each of us; we are forced, once again, to play our childhood selves. Some psychologist out there probably has a name for this phenomenon. The rest of us just know it as, "That thing that happens whenever I go back home."

This regression to past personalities might be the reason some families get together on holidays, and not so much the rest of the year. Holiday gatherings are safe for families because they are structured around traditions and time clocks. I can endure almost anything (and anyone) if I have a view of the exit.

When a family gathers at the end of the life of one of their own, there are no traditions and there are no time clocks. So on come the costumes and personas we wore as children. Who was bossy? Who was funny? Who was late? Who missed Christmas dinner altogether? In our case, this worked out okay. During Dad's hospice, we relied on the predictability of our personalities: we looked to someone for leadership; we looked to someone else for levity; we told each other, when speaking about someone else, don't take it personally; that's just how she is when she's tired.

"But I'm not like THAT anymore!" someone protests. Really? I know a guy who negotiates billion-dollar deals on acquisitions for a Fortune 100 company. Yet, when forced to go up against the tough negotiators who are his sisters, this guy is mush. Sense an oncoming train, anyone?

My mother used to plead, "Don't fight." My dad always asked, "Why would you put any energy into that? Why do you care?" It didn't help; as kids, we cared, and we fought.

Dying is like tinder tossed on the caring fire. If you ever cared before, this emotion can be magnified now. Dying can be serious and important. It can also be physical, emotional, and spiritual work. Providing hospice care to someone you love is especially challenging because it draws on every resource, pits brother against brother and neighbor against friend in round after endless round of "Now what?" Ultimately, you know you're all going to lose because, in the end, your loved one is going to be gone, and you will be left here on Earth asking, "Did I do the right things? Did I help enough? Did I catch every opportunity to care? Did I say everything I needed to say? Did we starve him to death?"

And the dynamics are further complicated by timing. While it is possible to predict timing with some accuracy, no one purports to be reading those tea leaves with perfection. We do not always know how long hospice is going to last, and the uncertainty of timing can wear people down even further. The stamina required to care perfectly is superhuman. A person needs a break now and then.

Our hospice team told us, "Go places! Live life!" Healthy people have outlets. Healthy caregivers take time to recharge. Healthy sibling caregivers cut each other some slack now and then. A walk alone through a museum or an afternoon at a football game... these are life-affirming activities, essential for maintaining health and reducing stress. Caregivers and patients who have permission to step away will come back refreshed and ready to play ball, ready to absorb and deflect and learn and give and take. Caregivers who spend their days and nights looking into the face of DEATH are wise to look away sometimes and think about something completely different: LIFE.

Deployed to provide hospice care for someone you care about, you report to duty with only what is inside of you. If what is inside of you is not several years of training in hospice care, you might do what healthy people tend to do: back out. Backing out is different from taking a break. Backing out is when you try to pay someone else to do what you are not schooled in. Also known as "passing the buck," backing out is a natural reaction. If I am trained as a pet therapist, and someone says, "Now, you're going to bake a cake," I might say, "Um, no." I might go on to ask, "Can't we buy a cake at the bakery?"

Providing hospice care is something you can pay other people to do for you, but this time, don't. Don't decline this invitation, because, whoever you are, you have been invited and you are qualified to participate. You are needed, you are able, and you are the right person for the job. Whoever you are, you belong where you are at this time, in this situation. And while there will likely be paid professionals around you, including doctors and nurses and social workers, the crucial aspect of hospice care has to come from you. Let the water pour out of your cracked pot, my friend, and see what beautiful wildflowers begin to grow. In the words of Jan, our hospice nurse, "You can do this."

It won't be the easiest thing you've ever done. You're going to need some inner resources. If your inner resource bank does not boast a strong balance of courage, courtesy, patience, and a curiosity for new experiences, reach deeply into your childhood and find it. Find the sense of adventure and the AWE that we all are born with. If you don't have a sense of humor, cultivate one. Quickly. Spend some of your quiet, anxious moments thinking about where you came from and who you are, really.

Oprah had a guest on one of her shows who proclaimed that, after age twenty-five or so, we each have the responsibility to parent ourselves. Childhood demons can be vanquished and omissions corrected when, as adults, we develop our own language of self-talk. As I understand the theory, you let go of the mistakes your parents made and start making mistakes of your own.

If I were to take on that exercise, if I were to start parenting myself, I would start with words my dad might have used, because no way could I parent myself as well as my dad parented me. He wasn't perfect. Not nearly. We didn't make things easy for him, either. Imagine screwing up every single day, and coming home to a parent who looks you over, picks up the pieces of all the damage you've done, and says, "I think I'll keep you." That is my LIFE story. What's yours?

Grace

Today I pass by the back staircase
on my way to apartment 204
The air is thicker in there
I know you are leaving soon
I am angry somehow, angry for the steps
This mountain we are climbing. Why?

I choose the slow ride up instead
Push number 2, the doors slide closed
Slower than the usual slow
The lift eternal. The doors yawn open
So slowly. Follow the carpet.

I dig around inside myself
For a crumb seed of Grace
Feels like digging for small change
In a very tight pocket
And not helping.
Any sense of knowing, experience, wisdom
Falls away and I am fading into
Myself at 12, 10, 4 years old

At 204, I turn the knob, a slight jingle, a push

I sit silent, wordless, in the backseat,
Eavesdropping on grownup conversations.
My parents are young, strong
And I wait, watch, raptly
Study every gesture, pause and utterance
Want to know exactly
Where we are going, what it's like,
When will we get there? How do we get there?
What happens next?

I try to shut the door behind me,
But it never does.
Someone reminds me, Turn the latch.
Focus.

Phone rings, toilet flushes, music,
Cookies, marbled salami, Diet Coke,
Orange sherbet dried on the counter.
Bouquet of blue sponges on white sticks.
I sense you then behind me—I know it's you—
Hands on my shoulders—
The way I knew you then—
Surprised me less then than now
In this place of in between
The feeling falls off in layers, a small soft hush
A shrug of melting snow

I pick a sponge stick and a book or two
Close my eyes
Inhale deeply
And walk into you.

Thank you, Dad, for a life well lived.
A journey well traveled.
So much to discover.
So much still undone.

-         Penny

Satisfied

By Brian

When told he was dying, my father said, more clearly than he had asked for breakfast or anything else for months, "I am satisfied." How does a person get there? How do you measure a life well lived? How, specifically, did Dad come to the completely correct conclusion that he did?

I know many are "satisfied" by achieving success in business. I guess this is measured monetarily or based on the level of recognition by others. By this measure, my father was certainly a success. He made much, although by his own admission he never worked a day in his life. He is in a "Hall of Fame." Guess that should do it. But it meant little to Dad. When informed he was selected to be inducted into that Hall of Fame, with tears in his eyes, he said, while the award would be meaningful, he was overwhelmed that his children had nominated him.

I know many people are "satisfied" by being a hero. I guess that is measured by risking one's life and receiving recognition. By this measure, my father was a success. He flew more than his requisite thirty-five missions during World War II and received a Purple Heart and a Distinguished Flying Cross. He watched his friends die as members of the Greatest Generation. He wrote a book about his wartime experience so others would know how it was. Yet, when any of his sons registered for the draft, he adamantly told them fighting in a war was something he had done and not something that defined who he was.

I know some people are "satisfied" by volunteer work and leisure. I guess that is quantified by passion for sport and recognition. By this measure, my father was a success. His children remember hours spent alongside him, not apart from him, on the golf course, and talking about golf at home. Even summer vacations were planned around an annual tournament in northern Minnesota that offered flights to accommodate every level of player on our family golf team. Dad received a Lifetime Achievement Award for his work with the Minnesota Golf Association and the USGA. Yet, among the biggest smiles and most genuine happiness I saw in my father was when he was laughing with his children and grandchildren as they bested him on the golf course.

In the end, we all define what we do in our own way. I think we all want to get to a point where, when we know we are going to leave this life, we are "satisfied." I actually think that statement may be the definition of happiness from the mind of some Greek philosopher three thousand years ago. So, how do we get there? How did Dad get there, if not through work or service or leisure?

I have thought about this a thousand times over the last decade as I attempt to define how I want to live as a human being in the world. What do I tell my kids about what may be this most important of questions? I think in the end, there are no words but truly only examples, and I can give a couple.

In his last days, around his last words to me, and among words I could not understand, my father said clearly, "I am fine as long as I have my People." It is something his sons and daughters appreciate; we understand deeply that there is a "person" and there are "people." We are Dad's People.

My father, rightly, loved and respected my mother above all other people and things. My mother is an amazing person, and my father has taught me the lesson that, in the end, the love of a man for his wife is the very basis for the love he has for others. This is an extremely important lesson that I think is too often marginalized and rarely passed down to children.

As for "the people," the eleven of us know very clearly that our father is "satisfied" because of his love for us. My father defined himself by who we have become and how we live. He often has been closest to us when we have had the most to be worried about. While I know I am the favorite, I know, also, that each of my siblings feels the same.

I know each of us completely understands the unmitigated joy, the jump in the heart, we have felt when seeing the smile and joy in Dad's eyes as he looked at our children and we realized that he loves them as much as he loves us. How unbelievably wonderful is that?

I guess if I am going to bother to write this, I ought to attempt to answer the original question: How did Dad understand he did things right? Here is my compulsion, in the form of advice to my children.

To my children: Your grandpa was a great man. He was great not because people told him he was great, nor because he received plaques and awards. Number 1, he was great because, without exception, he loved and respected his wife, your grandmother. He was and is also great because he lived a life well lived. He died "satisfied," and that, in the end, is all we can hope for. He taught all of us here, his People, that what that means is absolute, unconditional, unmitigated and loving love and acceptance of your family and those you love. You can have amazing success in a career, be a legitimate hero, and have balance across all aspects of your life—but, in the end, to be loved and, more important, to love, is what it takes to be Jack I. Moore and to be Satisfied.

Something You Carry with You

The day he received his cancer diagnosis, Dad told his family, "You should know, I haven't changed that much." When making decisions on his behalf, it was helpful to keep in mind the kind of person Dad was: what he was like now, but also the way he had been before age and illness found him.

Mickey once commented about how even-keeled Dad always was. She said, "If you think about it, it's not like nothing bothered him. He just had his priorities straight. He knew how to set his 'reset' button."

Where had Dad's life taken him, to teach him that? Was he born calm, cool, collected? Or was he made into that person by his experiences?

In retirement, Dad noticed the plethora of World War II movies that were becoming popular, and he felt there should exist a personal, factual record of what really happened during the second Great War. He had never talked much with his family about his Army Air Corps experience. By the time he married Mom, the war was ten years behind him. A kid snooping in Dad's closet, looking for a quarter or a bag of tees, might notice in his dresser drawer three rectangular blue boxes, hinged at the top, containing a Purple Heart medal and a couple others. That was about all we knew of the profound experience Dad had had eons before we became his theater and our teen years his battleground.

Dad graced his wartime memoir with both excitement and humor. His book was meticulously researched. If he remembered an incident, he researched until he had obtained documentation confirming that a plane had crashed, an entertainer had visited, or a certain food was served in just the size and color container that he remembered. His names and dates and explanations were accurate, and this was important to him.

Toward the end of his life, Dad enjoyed hearing us read to him from his book, telling us even through dementia and eventual Alzheimer's disease, "Yes, that's what happened. That's how it was."

My friend Marie, an actress, stopped in on Fridays to read from Dad's book to the residents at River Village. They were Dad's age. Their husbands and brothers and fathers had gone off to the same war. This was their story, too. They listened excitedly, nodding and murmuring, "Yes, that's what happened. That's how it was."

During a reunion of his bomb crew fifty years after the war, Dad participated in an impromptu interview with an historian and film crew as they followed the veterans through a hangar where B-24s and other relics of war had gone to rest. As Dad explained then, war is one of those things a person carries for a lifetime. Following are Jack Moore's comments, transcribed from that impromptu conversation.

We Were Needed

"We were needed," Dad said, "and it's something you carry with you. People who weren't there are never going to understand. You make a deal with your mortality. 'I'm never going to get home, so whatever happens is going to happen to all of our crew and that's the way it's going to be.' You don't really get uneasy until you get up there around thirty missions and you think, 'Hey, I might make this,' and then you start thinking about home.

"We never aborted. We flew every mission. We went to the target if we took off. And that was because of Chris Muller. I remember sitting in driving rain at the end of the runway and Jan running up the engines, with a full load of bombs and everything, and Jan turns around and hollers, 'Muller, the mags are falling off, what is this?' And Muller says, 'Ah, the leaves are a little wet, let's go.' So we did. It shows me we were absolutely dependent on each other. Muller said, 'Go.' The pilot didn't say, 'Well, let's take another look at it.' Nobody on the crew argued with anyone else. We all had our jobs to do. We did feel well trained and relied on each other. They talk about team spirit. It's something we never talked about, but it was there.

"[After the war] we went from one world into another. We had lived together for a year and a half, two years, gone through a lot of things, and at that point we were more of a family than you would expect to experience at any other time. But that had its uncertain elements, too. It wasn't all pleasure. So once it was over and we had survived it and went home, we went to a completely different world. And those people weren't really in that world. We didn't forget them, but we were busy doing things, going to school, getting married. And so, while you thought of them sometimes, you were too busy doing other things to take the time to go phoning around the country to see if one of these guys caught a cold or something.".

In the background, a reporter can be heard asking another question.

"Was I afraid?" Dad paused to think about this. "It's hard for me to explain. We did not expect to get through thirty-six missions. You hope to and you don't think, really, down in your heart, that anything is going to happen, but you're ready for it. I used to think, so I go down here over the ocean and the guys that goofed off at home are going to live another thirty, forty, fifty years and they're going to end up where I am, so I'm not going to worry about that."

Suddenly, Dad smiled, recalling a conversation. "I was talking to a flight surgeon over on Okinawa one day. We had almost finished our missions by then. He said, 'Well, you know, Jack I., once you guys get home, you're going to be really easy to please; a dish of ice cream, meet some interesting people.' And that's exactly right. I feel so grateful to God every day. I'm here and enjoying life to this point. I never thought that I'd live to be thirty or forty or fifty, but I did feel that, once I'd lived to be twenty-two, there was a good shot I'd live a lot longer."

TheWhen the interviewer asked what Dadhe took away from his wartime experience;, Dad's responseanswer was heartfelt and strong.

"You want to know what I learned? As far as flying the missions, we were a good crew. They kept picking us to lead things and so what I learned from that was an absolute interdependence that we have on everybody and it's true all through your life. I've owned businesses and you have to depend on other people. You have to believe other people and try to find people around you that are there for you and good in a crunch and I think we had that on this crew to a greater extent than we realized when we were doing it."

Could today's youth handle the same situation as effectively? Dad's response was one we'd heard before.

"As far as the young people now, I do think this and I think it very sincerely, that the younger generation is very, very much underestimated. It's just full of good people. They're meeting obstacles we didn't have to meet, doing more difficult things, trying to fathom technologies, trying to get into a position where they can really survive in what is a very competitive world. Sure, the economy is good now, but as they say in the Air Force, anybody can fly an airplane when it's straight and level, but what do you do when it flips on its back? And I think if the same situation arose, under the same circumstances, I have no doubt they would be really good, that they would perform in national life excellently."

In closing, the interviewer asked what Dad was feeling, standing beside a B-24, reunited with his crew.

"Seeing the crew is emotional to a certain extent. You know what it makes really clear to me, and I think it's something that's bothered all of us in the same boat for a long time, is that we lived in a different world. It was not a real world at all. We had experiences in that world that you can't understand. Nobody can understand if they weren't there. It's just that unless you were there, you know, been there, done that, and leaned on these guys and put your life on the line and come out on the right side instead of the wrong side, you're a different person.

"Sometimes people say to me, 'Nothing ever bothers you.' Well, what can bother me? What worse can happen that could have happened already and it didn't happen? So it gives you kind of—it levels you out. If you went into it and you got through it, it's better than a college education. It taught you how to live with people; it taught you how to meet yourself face to face.

"But like some other people say, 'War is a few million other men's hard luck.' And I weep for them."

Part III

Why Should I?

Our Hospice Story

I'm scaring the dog
My sadness a little loud
Siblings, here I come

Why Should I?

Dad's decline from golf cart to walker to wheelchair over just a few weeks' time sent our family on a health information scavenger hunt. Internet evidence led us to believe an infection was to blame. Tests for that proved negative; Dad's trusted internist thought it might be something else. He invited Dad to come in for a CT scan. Dad did not fully understand why he had to drink a pungent liquid; nor did he desire time inside a computed tomography scanner. He did cooperate, however.

After the scan, the doctor explained that he was looking for problems in Dad's intestines. He said he'd know more in a week or so, and that whatever it was could be handled over the phone. He recognized that taking Dad outside was problematic in what had become extremely cold weather, even for Minnesota, and we were glad to avoid it.

Expecting to wait for news, we were surprised when we heard from Mom later that night. The doctor had called and wanted to see Dad in the clinic the next morning. There must be a mistake, we said. Maybe the nurse didn't know the situation. Ask them to check with the doctor. Is there a chance that you misunderstood?

"No," Mom insisted. When Mom knows she is right, her pitch rises from patient to painful; her tone Nice Guy. shifts from friendly to fiery. "It was the doctor himself on the phone, not a nurse and not an administrative assistant. He wants to see Dad in his office in the morning and we are going to need a ride." All righty then.

The following afternoon, Terry e-mailed an update:

Mickey, Julie, Brian, and I joined Mom and Dad for the follow-up appointment at Dad's doctor's office today. It turned out to be a profound experience.

First the clinical. Dad has colon cancer. This is the cause of his weight loss. The good news is that there is no evidence of the cancer spreading. Therefore, Dad has two reasonable options: (1) surgery and (2) palliative (comfort) care.

Sparing much detail, surgery carries risks ranging from not surviving the operation to post-op infection and post-op psychosis. It might make his dementia worse. The best expectation from this option would be a week in hospital and a few more weeks in bed post-op. He would gain weight and might live another 3-5 years.

Palliative care would make Dad comfortable and let the cancer run its course. This would give Dad 3-6 months, maybe a year. Mostly comfortable, mostly at home. Bowel obstruction is a risk, which would mean pain and an immediate trip to the ER.

As usual, we talked about these options as if Dad were not in the room. When we asked Dad for his thoughts, he talked more than I have heard in months, and he was remarkably lucid. Brian explained Dad's options to him in stark terms. Dad's response was clear, although he missed a word now and then.

Dad said, "I am still Jack I. Moore. You should know," and he pointed to each of us in turn, "and you should know and you should know," and then he leaned around Mom to see Julie, and he pointed at her, "and you should know, I have not changed much."

He said he is "happy" and "satisfied." He wants to be at home with "you people." He understands that he is loved by many. When the doctor asked him directly if he wanted to have the surgery, he said, "Why should I?" He spoke with the strength of the dad of a year or two ago and with the peace of one who knows he is near the end and is all right with that. For what it's worth, the four kids at the appointment share that opinion.

No final decisions have been made, but a decision regarding whether or not to have the surgery should be made in the next two weeks. Dad does have a Health Care Directive, which must be considered. Meanwhile, a palliative care consult has been ordered.

When Terry's message arrived, Mickey and I were back at River Village with Mom and Dad. I read the e-mail aloud and, after a brief discussion, e-mailed a response to Terry:

Mom wants you to know that she believes the decision against surgery has been made. I am saying aloud what I am typing and when he heard Mom's comment, Dad's response was, "Those are the words that I put in."

Mickey has asked me to add, "Dad generously and clearly stated what he wants. That he is happy and satisfied. That he has tried to live a good life, that he loves us and that he feels lucky." Dad is nodding. Fascinating journey.

Simultaneously, from his law office across town, Brian shared a similar take on the situation:

I thought Dad did understand the circumstances and his words were to let us know he is happy with the life he has lived. Though never directly said, I do think he was telling us he is ready to go. I feel Dad was speaking as someone who knows he is going to die.

I welcome input from others, but believe Dad made his thoughts clear, in an incredibly beautiful, graceful way, with a peace that I can only imagine having when I am there. I found myself with tears because of the beauty and grace of what we saw, not with sadness. Crazy.

Listserv[3]

The minute word of Dad's diagnosis went out, the cacophony escalated; everyone had something to say. In response, Chris had the insight to construct an effective communications infrastructure. Over the next few weeks, "The Listserv" would become our go-to communication tool and our virtual talisman. It was a source of comfort through which we could reach the entire family care team anytime - and we did. People knew they could be contacted instantly through Listserv, and Listserv had the wisdom to string our random, intertwining conversations together chronologically, by subject.

Thanks to technology, Listserv is only one of many communications solutions available to families. Caring Bridge is another—popular and easy to use. The truth is, we chose Listserv because that's what Chris set up. When selecting a communications resource for your situation, the best way to connect is the way that works for your team. A few things to think about:

- How tech-savvy is your family? If you are already using a Facebook page or e-mail to communicate, perhaps you can stick with the familiar. Be patient with those who need to learn something new; it wouldn't be fair to leave

---

[3] Listserv was registered as a trademark with the U.S. Patent and Trademark Office in 1995, based on its use since 1986. It was registered with the Swedish Patent and Registration Office, PRV, in 2001.

someone out of these conversations just because he or she has limited computer experience.

- Who cares? Discuss the level of privacy your situation requires and the types of information that will (and will not) be shared. How much does the curious, unrelated public need to know?
- Boundaries? Conversations about one parent passing on can lead unwittingly to discussions about the financial situation of the surviving spouse. Although Listserv was reasonably private, we agreed to take this topic offline.

Chris' first Listserv message gave us a place to begin; we took our cues from his conversational tone and his encouragement. Those who said, "I don't get it," were quickly brought up to speed both out of necessity and because the tech knowledge required was pretty basic: click "reply," write a note, click "send."

What do people discuss in these situations? After explaining that the Listserv was functional, Chris' message went on:

> Dad and Mom are both sleeping. Dad is not uncomfortable, he is not in pain, just tired... which makes sense. He really likes crushed orange popsicles - like flavored ice chips - bring some when you can. He is eating and giving thumbs up (liked the cheese potatoes and strawberry shortcake) and thumbs down (lasagna didn't impress him). Most importantly, he is great at saying when he's had enough.

Like other families, the Moores imagine when we are together that our family is unique. Do other families jump into poetry as an acceptable means of communicating and coping?

We do it all the time. We quote, we craft, we mangle great works; we pay each other a dollar to recite a ridiculous limerick in public. Often, we read something aloud because it hits home and might resonate with others, as well. I think it is sometimes the raw simplicity of poetry that bears us across the extraordinary moments in our ordinary lives.

Maybe poet Elizabeth Alexander understood this, as she expressed in her poem, "Ars Poetica #100: I Believe":

> Poetry is what you find
> in the dirt in the corner,
>
> overhear on the bus, God
> in the details, the only way
>
> to get from here to there.

For our family, Listserv and the information, including poetry, we shared there, was our primary means of transportation. It was our only way to get from HERE (normal life, Dad, Mom, their People) to THERE (normal life, no Dad, just people).

When Are You Coming?

Ghost in the Room

Last night I was a ghost in the room
I could hear the phone fall on the floor
hold on to it, mister!
she laughs
say hello
she whispers
hello!
he says-
sounding like a man alone
in a canyon-
listening for the echo
I could tell
he could not see me
hellooo!
it's me dad
just saying hello
where are you
he asks
I'm not there
I say
but will be
he answers-
oh, that will be nice
I hear a door bell
then 3 small voices
hi, grandpa
hi, grandpa
hi, grandpa

I think they are hugging him but
I cannot see him
because there are so many angels

surrounding him
he is hidden now
in a forest of family
familiar faces from
then and now
those long gone
and those very present
encircle him now
I cannot see him
for all the angels
between us
I am not there
but we will be...
that will be nice.

-        Rob

When a guy is approaching his ninetieth year on Earth, sensible people recognize that the sand is running short in the hourglass. For out-of-towners, it's hard to judge the right time to cancel appointments, pack bags, board planes, and begin the final Goodbye.

Years before Dad's death, when Alzheimer's disease was just moving into our lives, Chris, Ellen, and Jackson were loading suitcases into the car, heading out to the airport after a holiday visit.

I asked Chris, "What if this is the last time you see him?"

"I think about that every time." Chris' shoulders drooped inside his leather jacket as he made another trek up the driveway, back into the house, for another suitcase, another goodbye.

"Where's Poppy going?" Chris' four-year-old son, Jackson, wanted to know.

"He'll be right back," Jackson's mom, Ellen, assured him, wrapping her arm around his little shoulders.

"That's good," replied Jackson, "because I want him to show me the Witch's Hat Tower on the way to the airport."

Age four or age forty, there will always be things we want our dad to show us along the way, and we get a little anxious when it seems our time together might be interrupted. We call, we visit. But this family, like many, stretches literally around the world, and for grandchildren overseas who had just welcomed a new baby into the clan, trekking to Minnesota in the middle of December was a nonstarter. On the other hand, for siblings within driving distance, it was a no-brainer. The question was timing.

Chris' suitcases were probably still open in a corner of his Manhattan apartment when he got Terry's e-mail about the cancer diagnosis. Chris' family had traveled to Minnesota for a summer wedding, and he had returned to act as Dad's personal care attendant for another family wedding in October. In his pocket were tickets to return after Christmas. Dad's prognosis at this point was three to six months, maybe a year. You could say that no one expected Chris to come running back twice between Thanksgiving and Christmas, but the fact that he did was not entirely surprising. After participating in the hospice meeting by telephone, he wanted to be on-site. What had he heard? What did he think?

We told Chris, it's not yet.

He answered, "I want to be there. I want time with Dad when Dad knows, on some level, that I am there." He reserved a seat on a plane and a guest suite at River Village, and he arrived on Friday for a long weekend in Minneapolis.

Rob was living nearer, a half-day's drive away in Appleton, Wisconsin and visited frequently. Rob's son attended college in Minnesota, and the two liked to join Dad for a Vikings football game together when it worked out. Like Chris, Rob's routine was to call Mom and Dad almost daily.

As Dad's demeanor changed and his activity level declined, telephone conversations with travelers picked up. One early morning, Mickey was giving Rob some updates and getting his thoughts on Dad's recent changes. After talking quite a while, Mickey asked Rob, "When do you think you'll be in Minneapolis again?"

He answered, "Mickey, I'm halfway there right now."

The Intake Meeting:
Another Stage of Loving

Our mom, Emily, breezed into the River Village conference room wearing a multicolored, hand-painted Uptown Art Fair sweater; she was wielding a postmarked white envelope in one hand and waving wildly with the other. One might imagine that a mother of almost a dozen children, a sweet and placid former schoolteacher, is naturally mild mannered. She can be. But there are other times...

Knowing that the intake meeting would include most of her adult children, she guessed correctly that getting a word or two in between her children's questions and comments would be a challenge. Ever the problem solver, she planned ahead, scribbled a few notes on the back of an envelope (I still have the original), and brought the meeting to order.

"I have something to say," she began. "Before we start, may I say a few words?" Of course.

We kids quietly listened to a story we had heard countless times before; it was the story of how our parents met. Mom wanted to share her perspective, to reassure us, to tell us that this was just another stage, another part of our life experience; everything was going to work out. Sitting tall, with our dad's hand on hers, she read:

I'm Here as the Mom

I'm here as the mom to thank you for your love and affection. I want to remind you this meeting is one of the stages of loving.

Almost sixty years ago, when Jack's nephew, Danny, said, "Jack wants to talk to you," I told Jack we ought to meet and satisfy everybody.

I said, "I've listened to your radio show. I'd like to meet you."

He asked, "When?"

"Let's get it over with," I said. "How about tonight?"

"Sorry," said Jack.

"How about tomorrow?"

"Okay."

Tomorrow came. We talked and talked... All these years later, now with our people, we are still talking. Now, another stage of love, of loving, for us all.

-        Emily

That sunny Saturday afternoon in early December, in the meeting room at River Village, a nurse and a social worker thanked Mom sincerely for her comments, and we all dove into organizing hospice services for Dad. The hospice team explained what hospice care is, what our responsibilities would be, and how expenses would be handled.

The nurse knew that Mom's health and safety would be critical to Dad's hospice success. If Mom became sick or injured, we would have two parents to care for.

"You're going to need help." The nurse was direct with Mom. "You cannot lift and move this man. Fortunately you live in a place where aides are available to help you. When he needs to get up, you need to call for help." Immediately, arrangements were made for aides to come in every two hours to take Dad to the biffy.

Next on the agenda: nutrition. Bottom line, let Dad decide. He shouldn't be forced to eat, nor kept from eating the foods he's hungry for. He would be allowed to have anything, no diet restrictions. The nurse explained that too much is more harmful than too little at this point. We were told to begin thinking about comfort as separate from food. Apparently she knew our family pretty well already. We grew up in a house where, when someone stopped in for a visit, the welcoming ritual involved Mom pulling every food available out of the pantry and fridge. Nice for college kids; less helpful to middle-aged weight watchers in the family.

We discussed dropping some of Dad's prescriptions. Eldest sister Mary is constantly studying nutrition, health, raw foods, and organic supplements. She expressed concern about reducing Dad's medications and vitamins. She stated emphatically that when her time comes, she wants her supplement regimen to continue. Okay, okay. But Dad's would not. Mary has always been keen on taking pills. Dad, not so much. The weaning would be coordinated by hospice with Dad's internist on the next business day. A Care Kit would be available if needed, containing the medications Dad might require down the road to manage pain and symptoms. This was the first time some of my siblings had heard about the Care Kit. It wouldn't be the last.

A twenty-four-hour nurse line would be available for anyone who had questions or concerns. Both the nurse and the social worker encouraged Mom to call.

"Call anytime," they said, "even in the middle of the night." They smiled and handed over a pile of brilliant neon stickers. "Here's the number, on these neon stickers." There were tons of them.

We had to ask the question on everyone's mind, and the hospice nurse was helpful, if vague. We told her the doctor had said three to six months, maybe a year. The hospice nurse's estimate, based on the progression of symptoms, was more like three months or less. Of course, no one could say for sure.

Suddenly, Dad spoke up. "I don't know what you all are talking about," he said.

Patiently, Mom explained what the meeting was about; as we listened, the rest of us were reminded that, first, Dad is still here, paying attention, and, further, he deserves the courtesy of being included in the conversation.

By the time the nurse and social worker left, the equipment Dad would need had been ordered, and delivery was set for later that day. Without realizing it, we were initiating River Village into hospice. Dad would be their first-ever hospice patient. This was Dad's home; it had never occurred to us that other residents went somewhere else to die. The social worker assured us they would handle all communication with the nurse there to coordinate Dad's care.

After the meeting, Lindy, third oldest and a natural leader, jumped on Listserv with her summary from the meeting, ending with the following:

> Very good meeting all around, with lots of discussion. Dad was present for the whole thing, seemed to listen, and seems to have an understanding of what is happening. Tighter hug than usual when I left.

Rob responded to Lindy's note with his usual humor:

> Excellent recap. Those are all the key points as I recall them. Lindy, please send Terry his list of assignments, including restroom reading attendant for all residents.
>
> On a more serious note: Once hospice starts getting more involved, they said they can give us a better idea about

length of time. They said sometimes one year turns out to be 2 weeks, and sometimes 2 weeks extends beyond a year.

Yesterday, Dad ate quite a bit and fed himself for the most part when they brought in lunch. Stayed up and alert in his chair through the whole game, though he wasn't overly interested in it. On the other hand, when he was getting ready for bed the other night, I was alarmed by how thin his legs are now. You guys all know this, but it is no wonder that he has difficulty standing and walking. I don't know how those legs can support him, even at his reduced weight.

I guess we all take this one day at a time, and pray that Dad remains comfortable and at peace with everything, and that Mom does, too. Please keep the updates coming. Thanks.

That meeting was as intense and emotional as any gathering we'd experienced; it went well, but it was tough. As the group dispersed, Mom and Penny conspired to make a brief escape of their own to the nail salon. Lindy agreed to bring Dad upstairs for a nap, and Mom and Penny snuck away. Poor Lindy.

While the boss-mom was out, and while Dad napped contentedly in the bedroom of the two-room apartment, Lindy heard a knock on the door. On the Memory floor, a knock on the door usually means a conversation with someone who is lost or confused. Although she probably considered it, Lindy never ignored a knock. She gingerly turned the knob and peeked through the crack in the slightly opened door.

This visitor was not a Memory floor regular. He was much younger, for starters, maybe midtwenties. He wore a

Twins baseball cap, and his plaid flannel shirt was hanging loosely over his jeans and tennis shoes.

"Hello?"

"I'm here with a chair for Jack Moore."

"Well, that was quick!" Lindy opened the door wider now, and saw that beside the delivery man was an oversized La-Z-Boy recliner, sent by hospice. Lindy knew it had been ordered. She didn't expect same-day delivery. She noticed the strange expression on the man's face and figured it had something to do with the presence of four or five blue-haired ladies lurking around him. He was tall, so they had to stand on their toes to see over his shoulders, to look into the apartment, to find out what would happen next. From the community movie room next door, swells of song from *The Sound of Music* billowed over the scene. "Come in," said Lindy to the man.

As Mr. Baseball Cap moved through the doorway, he gestured to the curious girls behind him. "Coming in?" he asked them.

"No!" Lindy exclaimed, a little too loudly, startling the man. "They don't live here."

"Sorry," he grinned. He carried the chair into the middle of the room.

"Can you help me move some of this furniture around so we'll have a place to put that?" Lindy asked.

"No, I'm sorry, I can't," he replied. He did move it near to where she wanted it, and then he and his cap headed out into the world.

Lindy stood with her hands on her hips, surveying the room. She had a lot of furniture to move, and no one to help her. She couldn't leave the chair where it was. And she had to finish this project before Dad woke up and wandered out to check on things. She rolled up her sleeves and got to work.

By the time Mom and Penny returned, their nails and their laughter bright, Dad was awake and appreciating the quality and comfort of his fine new chair. Finally, a quiet moment.

First Night with Hospice

A sense of relief and calm. We now knew as much as we were going to know; the train had chugged quietly out of the station on a new and different track.

"Look at this!" As Lindy thumbed through the hospice folder, she noticed an unusual note. It was a reminder, handwritten, with stars all around it for emphasis: "Remember to live life! Go places! Enjoy!" She slammed the folder closed and stood up.

"Let's go!" she exclaimed. She wanted to take Dad out, to live life, to go places, to enjoy. We settled on a movie. The plan was to head for the Heights. The Heights Theater, that is. Dad had been an usher there back in the day, and for nostalgia or budgetary reasons, they've retained the theater in its original glory, so the slanted floor, ornate lighting, and greasy popcorn remained pleasingly familiar to Dad, even on those days when nothing else felt familiar. He liked it. Mom would enjoy a diversion, too. It was cold outside, snowing and dark, and even though everything about taking Dad out was complicated by walkers, wheelchairs, icy sidewalks, and the Alzheimer's effect known as Sundowning, we were determined.

As we helped Dad into his winter coat and Irish woolen cap, we reminded each other, "The note says, 'Go places!' It's okay."

As we helped Dad call the elevator and worked our way to the lobby downstairs, Dad asked repeatedly, "Where are we going? What are we doing?"

"It's okay," we promised.

As we found a seat for him near the fireplace and asked him to wait while someone pulled up the car, Dad wanted to know, "Why are we sitting here?"

"It's okay, Dad. It's okay."

Dad was not demanding or angry. His tone was conversational. He felt safe, but he just could not get the upcoming event to stick in his mind. He was cheerful, open, and slightly confused. As someone left to get the car, a couple more siblings shook off the snow from their jackets and stomped their boots inside the front door. When we as a family feel worried about things, we gather, uninvited and unannounced. This was the first night of hospice care. We gathered.

"Whattup?" the new arrivals wanted to know.

"We're going out," Dad replied.

"Hello, there!" We were startled just then by a man who appeared out of nowhere, with a grin and a solid handshake for each of us. He was leaning on a cane. By the joy on his face and Dad's, clearly, the men knew each other.

The scene is now set: Snow tumbles down outside the picture window. Couches in front of the fireplace. Mom and Dad side by side, a grandkid sprawled across a deep comfy chair near them, tapping on a tiny screen. Others standing around in scarves and heavy coats, an elderly man leaning on a carved wooden cane. No one else, really. Evening comes early to a place where dinner begins at 4:30 p.m. We had been instructed to go places, live life, enjoy. We were trying.

The man with the cane offered his right hand to Dad and winced in fun when Dad squeezed too hard. They exchanged the smile of ancient friendship, although their acquaintance had to be relatively new—a couple months, a year maybe. There aren't a lot of men in a typical senior residence; they tend to stick together.

The man said he was taking a trip, leaving the next day. He would be gone for a few weeks. Africa. Time passed, snow fell; someone's car was still idling out front. The happy man and his cane shuffled on.

"It's really comfortable here," someone remarked.

"We are supposed to go places," someone replied, adding, "This is a place."

"Yes, this is a nice place," chirped Dad.

Our plans quietly evolved. Dad stayed in the lobby with Lindy and Rob, who would bring him upstairs later on. Some siblings, seeing that all was well, went back to the world outside. A few accompanied Mom to a movie. As usual, we had followed directions while choosing our own—Dad's own—best path. Going someplace was rejuvenating for everyone that night.

With family as close as the next Listserv, updates were frequent and included whatever anyone wanted or needed to share: sometimes serious, sometimes humorous, mostly just FYI. Saturday night, my update was about movies and toilets and funerals. All equally important topics. Capitals in the message were intended to alert the speed-readers in the family that something pertained to them, specifically:

> Mom and Rob and I talked awhile after Dad went to sleep. The commode arrived, which Rob was kind enough to try out before the delivery guy left. Might need to be adjusted but seemed okay for Rob. The wheelchair arrived. It's a red version of the other one. BRIAN, do you want to return the wheelchair you rented for the wedding? Or maybe sell it to Sharon since her kids seem somewhat accident prone (how's the knee, Sharon? And whose knee was it?).
>
> Mom is thinking about a funeral. I did not initiate this part of the conversation—it is on her mind. She feels she

no longer knows many people at St. J's. She has reached out to someone about joining St. H's, but has not yet heard back.

MICKEY, she really feels welcome at St. Peter, but knows you're no longer active there. So no concrete direction to go but realize this is on her mind and on her list of things to take care of. She is also thinking about last rites. She wants Father Bill (BRIAN, please call) and Father Kevin (MICKEY, please call) to visit Dad.

That's all. Mom and Dad seem settled into this, calm.

Three Months? Or Less?

We thought, three to six months, maybe a year. We thought, one more Christmas morning, one more birthday brunch, two high school graduations, more readings from Dad's book, more painting classes, more Masses, one more time hiding the Family Egg on Easter Sunday, one more wedding anniversary, Mother's Day, Father's Day, maybe two more Christmas mornings…

At the intake meeting, we were brought down to Earth with a sobering, "three months or less," based on the progression of Dad's symptoms. We never heard the "or less." We heard three months. Three months? Okay, one more Christmas for sure, one more birthday party for Dad and his brother, Bill, and granddaughter, Maureen, to share, playoff football, high school hockey, possibly one more Easter.

Phrases such as "or less" do not apply to optimists.

Monday

Beginning one Monday in mid-December, the phrase "or less" began to spin in our ears like a broken record, or in the irritating way that a truck's reverse warning signal grates on the brain when the beep beep beep beep drones on too long. Chris had spent a weekend at River Village, relieved and satisfied that he had made the decision to come. He was deciding whether to return before or after Christmas.

"I think you should stick to your plan," I told him. "You already have tickets. You know you'll be here in a week and a half. Spend Christmas with your family. We will text you if there's a change and you can get here if you have to. The hospice nurse will give us lead time if she can. They know all the signs."

Chris felt conflicted. How to be everywhere? And if this went on for three months, as we hoped, then did it make sense to keep running back and forth?

"He knows you want to be here," I told Chris. "It was so great that you came now, when you could really communicate and have some good time together."

It was a nonconversation, because Chris clearly wanted to be in two places at once and I didn't know what to tell him. It was such a tough call. He passed through the sliding doors at the airport still looking over his shoulder.

Tuesday

Tuesday, Brian began to wonder about Dad's timing. He had just been through hospice with his father-in-law and he had his own ideas about the changes we were starting to notice. After a quick check in Tuesday morning, he resolved to stop in every day on his way to work.

Sharon stopped in Tuesday night:

> Diego and I were at Mom and Dad's tonight. Mom seemed upbeat. Dad was sleepy and stayed in bed. When he woke, we visited a little. I asked if he wanted to rest. He said, "Yes," so I covered him in a blanket and we chatted with Mom, Lindy and Penny. He clapped and smiled when he saw Diego—very cute. Want to spend as much time with him as possible.

> I saw Chris' request for rosaries. I have two rosaries in my purse and one on my rear view mirror; I can leave one for him next time I'm there. I didn't see the prayer book but will look for it. Would have been nice to read to him while he rested.

Wednesday

Brian called me Wednesday morning, "Are you going to the place today?"

"Maureen and I stopped by yesterday and I thought we'd go tomorrow night." In other words, wasn't planning to.

"How was Dad when you saw him?" Brian asked.

"Tired." I explained that we had arrived at four and Dad had been asleep all afternoon. Father Bill had been by earlier with Communion. Mom seemed calm. The whole place seemed peaceful in an eerie kind of way.

I went on, "When we were ready to leave, Dad saw Maureen standing in the living room. He waved to her and smiled. We went into the bedroom and said Hi. I asked Dad if he wanted to sit in the living room and he said, No. He just seemed really comfortable with the blanket pulled up under his chin, really smiling."

I reminded Brian that Anna was in town, too, and maybe hanging out there today. I made every excuse for not going back that day, for taking a day off, because the rest of life seemed to be calling me. And I felt all of the guilt of not going, even knowing that no one has to be there every minute, that it is really okay to let others step in.

"Can you just go over there?" Brian asked.

"Sure, but why?"

"I think Dad's dying." Understand, Brian can be as sentimental as the next guy, but he is not an alarmist. He was looking for an honest impression about what he felt was a dramatic change. Some people get what they want because they know when to ask. Brian is one of those people.

I called my office and explained that I would be going AWOL for a while. I said, "I don't know, but my brother is concerned, so I told him I'd stop over there. If he's right, then I might disappear for a while. I just want you to know what's up."

The person I spoke with had lost his father recently and said he understood. He said, "Whatever you need. I get it. I had that last call four times."

"Let's hope I get four of these." Truth was, I, too, had seen a pallor over Dad that I couldn't ignore. I changed from a business suit to jeans and a sweater and picked up chocolate shakes on the way to River Village.

Brian's update that day was ominous:

> I visited Mom and Dad early this morning. Mom said she was awakened last night by a gurgling sound coming from Dad's throat and chest. She got a nurse; they changed his position and he coughed up phlegm. He was very cold to touch and they covered him with blankets. When I got there, Dad was sleeping. He woke up and we had a nice talk, although he never sat up. He was comfortable but closing his eyes often. Mom tried to give him a sip of water, but he could not swallow it and coughed quite a bit.
>
> The hospice nurse came at 10:30. Mickey and Julie were there. Mickey said that the hospice nurse made it clear that Dad's condition is progressing and showing signs of entering its final stages, but she did not see death as within hours or the next couple of days. A doctor will visit Dad later this week or on Monday.
>
> Mom is doing well and I am amazed how peaceful she is. Dad was in good spirits. I understand from Mickey that he remained upbeat the rest of the morning. I plan to visit again each morning. Will talk to you all tonight, but I thought the events of last night and this morning warranted a quick update via Listserv.

Wednesday night, I parked my car under a flickering yellow light in the parking lot at Lifetime Fitness, dialed into a conference call with my siblings and began planning Dad's funeral. It didn't seem real. Yet.

Thursday

On Thursday morning, I called Brian for an update, and went back to River Village with my kids in the evening.

"You need to spend time with Grandpa," I told them.

"Is he going to die soon?"

"Nobody knows. But he does love to see you guys."

Friday

My mother-in-law wakes every morning and says, "One more day, Lord! Thank you for one more day!" Friday was one more day. Lindy's daughter, Jamie, brought her infant son, Dylan, to River Village and Dad loved it. Wrote Jamie:

> He was sitting in his chair and said, "Bring that baby over here!" Dylan sat on his lap and it melted my heart! Later, as we were leaving, I gave him a hug and said, "I love you, Grandpa." He pulled me in close to him and said, "I love you, too." It meant the world to me to have those moments.

On Friday afternoon, I was driving to Michigan and called Mom from the road. She relayed the details of what would prove to be an unforgettable conversation with the doctor from hospice. Even months after Dad's death, Mom, who calls me on August 30th of every year and asks if this is my birthday (it isn't) would recount her afternoon with the hospice doctor as if it had happened just minutes ago.

"The doctor talked with Dad and checked him over," Mom explained. "He spent a lot of time doing that. Then he asked me to sit down with him in the living room. Rob was there, and some of the others. The doctor sat across from me and asked me how long I thought Dad had left to live."

Here, she paused. I waited. After a moment, in a controlled voice, she went on.

"I told him, two or three weeks." Yes, of course, that's what we all thought.

"And?"

"And," Mom spoke deliberately, careful to enunciate each word. "He looked me right in the eyes and said, very seriously, 'No. Two to four days.'"

Two to Four Days

All the Crazy Light

It was only
In your weakness
That you could not hide
Your strength
In a dim
And quiet room
At this small hour
Shines all
The crazy light
Doctor this
Doctor that
No matter;
You will go when
You wish
At your signal
We will get
The window
And no darkness
Shall follow.

–   Rob

Day One: Hard to Swallow

"Did we starve him to death?" After Dad's death, this nightmare took over my sister Mary's mind and held it hostage for days. She had to ask.

The answer was, definitively, "No, we didn't." Food can be a confusing piece of the hospice puzzle. Remember, the professionals tell us:

> The person may have a decrease in appetite and thirst. The body will naturally begin to conserve the energy which is expended on these tasks. Do not try to force food or drink into the person, or try to use guilt to manipulate them into eating or drinking something. To do this only makes the person much more uncomfortable. Small chips of ice, frozen Gatorade or juice may be refreshing in the mouth.
>
> If the person is able to swallow, fluids may be given in small amounts by syringe (ask the hospice nurse for guidance). Glycerin swabs may help keep the mouth and lips moist and comfortable. [Decreased appetite] may indicate readiness for the final shut down.

Knowing that food was going to factor in as a barometer during his last days, we became hyperfocused on Dad's appetite. It turned into something like a Pope watch, staring at the chimney, waiting for the smoke to change from black to white. We noted every sip and nibble and discussed every bite over Listserv. Did we imagine there was a correlation between nutritional intake and life span? Yes, truly. As long as Dad was eating, he was not dying. Yet. That said, we did not want to cause him discomfort. Listserv conversations discussing food reflected our concern. Did we starve him to death? Not even close.

Dad seemed in great energy this morning and asked about the snow.

He enjoyed the cinnamon raisin toast. Took his pills drinking from a sippy cup. He is able to communicate what he wishes to eat. Mom is not pushing food or drink.

He likes having "his people" around so stop by when you can. Bring a few orange popsicles if you think of it.

-   Chris

...noticeably weaker than even one week ago and he did not want to eat even the slightest amount of Jell-O or pudding - it looked to me like it hurt to swallow... Dad is having trouble talking & swallowing. Maybe hospice nurse can look at his throat?

-   Terry

Hospice nurse commented to me about the trouble Dad is having with swallowing. She said the body is really smart, and it shuts down the parts that would sustain it. The swallowing thing is one way we understand that Dad is at the beginning of the process. We noticed that he is reaching at his throat a little bit. Of course, he will not complain.

-   Mickey

Around this time, I welcomed a phone call from a friend, a medical doctor.

"Is he eating?" she asked.

"He wants to eat, he seems to have an appetite, but he has trouble swallowing. We don't want to force him to eat."

"That's right, but if he is not in pain and if you can keep him hydrated, you might have more time. He won't live forever, but maybe you can get him to Christmas, or until the family is all there." She suggested thicker consistencies, rather than thinner. More like baby food. She explained, in medical lingo, that water slips down the wrong way and can get into the lungs. She recommended a specific product that could be added to juice to create a consistency he could handle.

"He might really enjoy a chocolate shake," she added. Bingo! It was a prescription we could appreciate because we already knew about the magic of chocolate shakes: the breakfast, lunch, and dinner of champions.

We didn't starve Dad to death. We offered sherbet, shakes, and applesauce as long as he wanted them, and when he no longer wanted any he let us know by holding his hand up or by turning his head away.

Overall, comfort was a cryptoquip. We peered into our Dad's flinches and sighs and tried to uncover some meaning. We trusted whatever Mom suggested, even as we made our own assessments, measuring every mannerism Dad had ever had against his current behaviors.

In the living room, just outside Dad's bedroom, we held salons, discussing and remembering and comparing a lifetime of notes about this person we'd always known, this man who raised us. "He always did that thing with his wrists before a putt," and, "I remember seeing the same expression on his face when he would stand in front of the window looking out at the golf course," and, "He used to raise his eyebrow like that when I asked him for money."

Our conversations were all over the place. Someone commented, "Dad always seems to be reaching for something in his pocket."

That subtle reaching movement triggered the memory of the dad of our childhood who, when he needed a moment to think, would reach into his pocket to jangle the rosary there; he never revealed the secret string of beads, but silently rummaged them in his pocket.

Chris sent a note out on Listserv:
Everyone, bring rosaries!

Lindy replied:
Maybe, but he might also be looking for the handkerchief he also used to keep in his pocket.

Chris' next request:
Everyone, bring hankies!

What Dad needed was anyone's guess, because he wasn't going to explain his affectations to us. We learned to love and comfort Dad without food. We played music, read books, and chatted around him as we offered whatever we thought would bring Dad peace. Although he had always been an avid fan of television, the TV was not of much interest to Dad in the end. Maybe it was difficult to focus, or to hear the audio over the din of his kids' chatter. Ultimately, music seemed to satisfy best of all. Dad was enormously pleased by his musical grandchildren: Brock's guitar jam sessions, Jesse's songs and Jacob's recordings, the high-pitched whine of Kayla's violin, which he called her "machine," and the amazing musical gifts of his friends, Janet and Charles.

Mickey left a book of prayers in case anyone wanted to read them to Dad. Sometimes, Mom and Dad just sat there holding hands. Holding hands. How simple is that? Sharon wrote:

> I was holding Dad's hand at the end of our visit. I was glad I did and would recommend it.

One afternoon, granddaughter Molly described playing a song she had downloaded, an old favorite of Dad's. She told us,

> He immediately smiled and yelled, "Emy!" to have her by his side while they listened. To make it even more special, I sang a little along with the chorus and, when it was over he said, "Thank you."

"Thank you," at this time was an enormous gift. Dad wasn't able to communicate the way he once had, and this simple expression arrived fraught with meaning. It said, "I hear you," and "I appreciate your effort." It said, "This works for me," and "I love you." That little phrase was a big deal, and it was not lost on any of us.

A day or two after Molly's karaoke moment, when Dad was no longer leaving the big bed, I thought he might not mind a song. I sang a couple bars of something he used to enjoy, and Dad reacted by turning his head away from me, toward the window. We all have gifts. One of mine is not an ability to carry a tune in a basket. So, when he turned away, I stopped singing and laughed, casually remarking, "You don't like when I sing."

He turned his head back toward me and looked raptly into my eyes. I don't remember ever being locked in with Dad so intently. When he knew he had my attention he said, clearly and firmly, "Yes, I do."

As an aside, that brief exchange turned out to be something of a gift. After Dad had been gone awhile, my siblings were discussing their grief: the tears, the lost sleep, the memories they had of their relationships with Dad. I knew Dad loved me. He was my dad, after all. We had had some fun, I had helped him along the way, and he had certainly helped me. But I didn't have the symptoms my siblings were describing. I didn't mind. It was a simple observation that I accepted in my head the way I accepted that I would never be performing on *American Idol*. The thought that formed in my mind was that maybe Dad and I didn't have the same relationship he had with the other kids. This was not a thought based in self-pity. A guy who has almost a dozen unique personalities to care for will love all of them, but might naturally have more of an affinity toward some than others. Maybe Dad didn't like me the way he liked some of them.

How wrong could I be? As quickly as this thought was fashioned in my brain, a familiar voice responded, clearly, firmly, silently, from some distant place behind me and yet from within me, too. The voice said, "Yes, I do."

Through hospice, we discovered the many ways we could comfort Dad and one another, even without food or drink. When Dad did pass over, it was the crooning of Nat King Cole, and not the River Village lasagna, that accompanied him.

Day Two: Should Something Happen

Should something happen, you will all be notified. Out of respect, please DON'T post to Facebook. Those who can't be here deserve this much.

-        Molly

Why is it that, when Elvis leaves the building, everyone who would give anything to watch him go is waiting at the wrong door? We were not all where we wished to be at this point in the story, but we were connected.

Granddaughter Paree was in Ohio. She wrote:

A lot of thoughts are going through my head in Ohio. Especially, an appreciation of our shared stories and poems and of our family. The thought of drifting apart is devastating when what I've seen is a coming together and the value in that.

I have thought a lot about Grandma. To her, it's never about her, which is one of the most admirable traits. I've come to appreciate and respect that immensely in recent years. I feel far away, but I hope and pray that we all remain close.

Granddaughter Erin, whose husband, Matteson, was stationed in North Carolina, sent a note:

Dear Grandpa and Grandma,

Wish I could be there with you all. I miss you and the MN chill. Grandpa, I hear you're comfortable, cozy, and well taken care of. But of course you are; you've got Grandma!

To you both, Matteson and I want to wish you all the love you've wished us over the last year. Having you at our wedding meant so much. Thank you for making it. I know it was a trek (and man, the Basilica has SO many stairs)!

Grandpa, your stories on war and friendship and valor have been invaluable to Matteson.

Grandma and Grandpa, I have learned so much watching the two of you dance through life together. We both have. Thank you for sharing your gifts with us.

Cheers to my first Popsicle (GRANDMA!), to the great music (Grandpa), to the incredible family you've given me/us (Mom, Uncle B, Chris, Rob, Terry, Aunt Mic, Sharon, Lindy, Penny, Mary, their spouses and allll my favorite cousins).

Matte and I miss you both! Have a happy wintry day. See you soon.

Love,
Lil E

Erin's cousin, Anna, had lived in the red house while attending a high school for gifted artists. During that year, Dad taught Anna how to golf, and Anna taught Mom the technical skills to create stained-glass artwork. She had stayed close to them both, and accepted the gift of a friend's frequent flyer miles to be with her grandpa before he died. She knew this would mean she might miss his funeral, but being with him now mattered more to Anna and pleased her grandparents, too. After her visit, she returned to engineering school on the West Coast and wrote on Listserv:

Back to life. It isn't the same here in the Pacific Northwest. As pretty as the dull gray sky can be with mountains in the background, I wish I was crammed with y'all in that magical place. Give Grandpa one more kiss for me.

In response to Anna's e-mail, Mickey wrote:

Anna, Amazing to be able to look across the big bed and see your sweet face. You mean the world to all of us. Thank you for coming and sharing your grampa love. I hope the holy water cocktail serves you well this holiday season.

Holy water what? Penny, Anna's mom, had brought water from Lourdes, that sacred place in France where people can purchase key chains and postcards and chocolate-covered rosaries while being cured of all their afflictions. Coke bottles and milk jugs and mason jars lined the kitchen counter in the apartment and stood sentry in the window—all full of crystal-clear, blessed French spring water. Was Anna drinking that stuff? We each did whatever we felt was right and good, whatever we thought would help Mom and Dad during this challenging time. Maybe Anna was onto something.

Anna's sister, Leah, shared a memory and the lyrics from a tune she and Dad both enjoyed, agreeing that Ella Fitzgerald's version of the oft-covered song was best:

Easy to Love

I know too well that I'm
Just wasting precious time
In thinking such a thing could be
That you could ever care for me
I'm sure you hate to hear
That I adore you, dear
But grant me just the same
I'm not entirely to blame for
You'd be so easy to love
So easy to idolize all others above
So worth the yearning for
So swell to keep every home fire burning for
We'd be so grand at the game
So carefree together
That it does seem a shame
That you can't see your future with me
'Cause you'd be oh, so easy to love

Another grandkid, Cliff, had flown in from Oregon and now took up residence in the guest suite on River Village's first floor. His stay was indefinite. Cliff had spent years living with Grandma and Grandpa, and his close relationship with them was familiar to all of us. It was something he had always appreciated and often mentioned. This week, he became an honorary sibling, afforded all related privileges and responsibilities. His personal objective was to ride in the cars of every aunt and uncle during his stay, and he gave this a spirited effort.

Chris would arrive Saturday. I planned to be back on Sunday. Various others were scattered across Minnesota. Everyone's tin cans were strung together via Listserv. The words *two to four days* are especially impactful coming from a medical professional. It was time and we were ready: as prepared as we could be, if we had to be.

By Saturday afternoon, Listserv was lit up with updates, anecdotes, and, mostly, poetry. It was a way to be connected, and to be honest, and to be hopeful. In the words of Emily Dickinson,

Hope is that thing with feathers that perches in the soul and sings the tune without the words and never stops—at all.

We were incessantly hopeful.

Day Three: Everybody Wants In

"You live somewhere else," we told her.
"It's okay. I work here," she explained.
So she does.

Virginia, our personally anointed Patron Saint of Memory Care, appeared in Mom and Dad's bedroom on their first night on the Memory floor. She had tapped on the door and found it unlocked. My parents awoke to see the tall, ashen stranger standing like a holograph at the foot of their bed, her white, full-length nightgown gleaming in the white-yellow moonlight beside the open window. In lieu of curtains, behind the figure was likely a -star-studded midnight sky. Long dress, flaxen hair; she She could have been heading to the Oscars. She was lost.

"You don't live here," said our mother. "I'll take you home." The lock clicked into place but the tapping continued.

We had heard about Virginia, but during Dad's hospice we saw her in action, trying the door, daily, nightly. Someone always turned the knob to tell her gently, "You don't live here."

"It's okay," was Virginia's confident response. "I work here." So she does. During Dad's hospice, Virginia was a ghost messenger, pacing the Memory floor, tapping, tapping, peeking inside. She wore that ruffled, high necked, snow white gown day and night, and had a river of red-brown hair, the hair Dad's sister, our Aunt Pat, might have worn as a girl. Aunt Pat, deep in her own Alzheimer's disease, couldn't say goodbye to Dad herself, so she must have sent Virginia by proxy.

As Dad's lighthearted sister would have wished, Virginia brought the gift of levity, an excuse for us to look away from our father in his bed, any breath perhaps his last, and attend someone else for a change.

The unlocked apartment door was no surprise to our family. The big red house where Dad and Mom raised their family had no keys. Zero keys. Custom built for a family of thirteen, this house had every amenity available in its day. This house had a trash compactor, a microwave, two dishwashers, a library, an office, multiple living rooms, Atari, a VCR, a pool table, and a foosball table. This house had a kitchen table special ordered from an office supply store. This house had a smart intercom system and a dumbwaiter. But no keys. Dad was a person who lived life with his door unlocked.

At Dad's funeral, the grandchildren were amused, if not surprised, by the number of people they met who said, "I used to live at the red house." Some meant they spent a lot of time there, hanging out, watching sports, sitting around the kitchen table. Others meant, literally, that they had moved in. Someone whose family moved during her junior year, someone caught in his parents' tough divorce, grandchildren who needed a place to stay.

"Mom," one of us asked, "did the parents of those kids make arrangements for them to live with us?"

"No."

"Did you know how long they were planning to stay?"

"No."

"Did they pay you for expenses or anything?"

"No."

"?"

"We never talked about it," Mom explained. "We had plenty of room and they were kids we knew. They were always respectful, and they were busy working and going to school.

No, we never talked to their parents. It was fine. If it wasn't, they would have had to leave. But it was always just fine."

Sunday afternoon saw a thaw in Minnesota's black ice, and humans began to creep out of hibernation. People who loved Dad but had lost touch over the years had an opportunity to visit. From his bed, he greeted each visitor with a familiar grin, genuinely joyful to receive each guest. There were priests and chaplains and neighbors and cousins and Dad's brother, Bill. There were aides, nurses, and friends. They all wanted one more piece of Dad, wanted a moment to greet Mom and share a laugh or a memory. There were grandchildren and great-grandchildren, babies being tripped over, and food packed tightly into the fridge. There were people who knew just what to say, and others who hadn't really thought it through. Within the crowd, friends who hadn't seen each other in ages exchanged greetings across the big bed, handshakes, and smiles, while Dad just looked on, grinning. It was fine. If it wasn't, they would have had to leave. But it was. It was just fine.

Late Sunday evening, as the last nonrelative punched an escape code into the security keypad and left the Memory floor behind him, Mickey clicked the lock to Mom and Dad's apartment into place and turned to face her exhausted siblings. She leaned heavily against the door and the Christmas bells hanging from the knob jingled, barely. Mickey looked at us and proclaimed, "From now on, family only." And that was just fine, too.

Everybody Wants In

Slowly the door creaks open
The shadowy Ghost of Christmas Past peers in
"Not now, not here," we say

Coming down the hall I meet the sweet little Ghost of
Christmas Yet To Come
Eagerly she seeks admittance with her eyes

He was always a collector of characters
Bemused appreciator of wayward souls

Tonight as we open the window
Forgive us if we close the door
For we are Christmas Present

-        Mickey

Day Four: Family Only

Day Four, time froze. We were caught up with each other's anecdotes; we were done asking questions. We were wearytired of small talk and freshwe were out of inappropriate jokes. Reality settled over the apartment, leaving us all mostly head down, texting. Many of those texts went to our shared Listserv, even when we were sitting close enough to read the texts as they were being written, close enough to smell the lotion on the author's hands and certainly close enough to speak our thoughts aloud. We composed on tiny keyboards; it seemed no one could ever get the wireless service to work on a laptop in that apartment, although Lindy never gave up the quest.

Body language experts view texting as a nonpower pose. When a person communicates on a phone or an iThing, it is often with a closed posture: slightly hunched forward, both hands locked on a small object in front of him, making the person seem small, closed off, nonthreatening... powerless. Was our texting a way to admit that we were defenseless in this crisis? Or was looking down at a text message a way to escape the immediate surroundings, if only momentarily? Was crafting poetry a self-imposed therapy?

Whatever. The following snippets are what hospice looked like when it was, finally, only family:

The Head of the Clan

The head of the clan known as Moore
His faith shapes him down to the core
As gently and right
Jack moves on to the light
With the angels to sing and to soar!

                    –   Terry

His Wife

There is a mother in the mix
A wife
A light there too
And bright
Yet with a pang that sears
I see that she
When he goes
Is only one
Hey Emy! away
From going too

                    –   Julie

Gifts

How pleasing it must be
For the author to know
His precious people
Honor his spirit
Sharing words
As his soul transitions
His gifts remain
And we write on

-        Mickey

Standing Outside

Darkness and distance
An angel tap tapping the pane?
Never said goodbye

-        Julie

Can't Sleep

If a person is online at 3:41 a.m.,
is it mandatory to post, "Can't sleep"?

"Are there any updates?" Looking over our Listserv correspondence, I noticed that this question came from every one of us at some point, often in the wee hours, and that the one who answered was not always the person in the room with Dad. "Any updates?" was sometimes just a question, and sometimes a way to say a lot more than that.

Dec 17, at 3:43 am
Is there an update?

Dec 17, at 4:26 am
Very quiet all night.
Meds every 2-3 hours.
Almost zero fidgeting.
Mom showered and visited with Rob
awhile and she had some laughs
with Cliff and Mary and Lindy.
Hospice nurse comes Monday.

Lost:
Lindy left her phone on the
counter; resenting that blunder
Found
Now at home... have my phone...
I have to have the thing Just hope it doesn't ring!

Dec 17, at 5:43 am
What did I miss?

Dec 17, 6:54 am
What you missed was when Mom smooched up
Dad all over his cheek. He asked, What are you trying to do?
She said, I am kissing you. He said, I love that.

Dec 17, at 7:45 am
That's about the coolest thing I've ever read.

Dec 17, at 7:48 am
Chris is reading to Dad. We have given him (Dad, not Chris) two
drops of something to help cut through the secretions in the
back of his throat. Sometimes this morning he looks kind of
halfway into the distance and gets a giant grin. It seems like a
look of amazement. He seems relaxed.

Dec 17, at 9:47 am
I am working but will be there around 2:00. I work
nearby and I'll come if I am wanted or needed sooner.

Dec 17, at 9:51 am
I would love the updates to keep coming this
morning.
I am at work also but plan on coming after work.
Please let me know what you would like me to bring.

Dec 18, at 12:25 am—Midnight Blessings

May the night angels find you sometimes
Under satin sheets on a bed beside your lover
Staring at the ceiling, counting sheep

And may they tend to you, too,
When you are shivering under ordinary throws
On a chair beside your loved one
Staring at the heavens, counting blessings

Dec 18, at 3:14 am

We are waiting for no one
We are all here
In text lines and flashes
Of sky and moon
We surround you like air
The first to touch you
To learn your song
without the words

Dec 19, at 1:33 am

Dad is feverish. We are opting for the cold wet
washcloth to bring down his temperature, as Mom
always did for us. Listening to the steady rhythm
of Dad breathing and Mom snoring, I should be
able to catch up on several days' e-mail.

Dec 19, at 4:42 am

Sounds like another quiet night. Anymore?

Dec 19, at 5:18 am

A quiet night in Lake Wobegon. Some of you
will wake to see that the night angels have
invited you to a game of Words with Friends.

(Sent from a tiny keyboard)

Day Five: What Are You Waiting For?

On Day One, we accepted our task, Dad's fate. Days Two and Three, we begged for more time. Day Four, we were grateful for every extra blessed moment, but began to wonder when.

Rob reminded us, "Dad never hurried anywhere in his life." Rob was right. No golf course ranger in America could get Dad to tee off sooner or to putt faster. He would play out his round in his own time, and we wanted nothing else on his behalf.

On Day Five of Dad's two to four days, we foolishly tried to be brave and facilitate the finale.

"Let's leave him alone; he likes to be alone sometimes," someone suggested. Mom stayed on the big bed (*Alone* and *Without Emily* are two different things) while the rest of us stepped out.

Nothing happened. And we were grateful. But we didn't wish to hold Dad back.

"Let's open a window."

"Close that window! It's freezing in here!" No cryogenics for us.

I yanked a couple Christmas gifts out from under the tree. I don't think I believed this was the thing Dad needed to finish his last chapter, but it seemed as good a diversion as any.

"Dad, are you waiting for your Christmas presents?" Mom opened Dad's book for him first, a photo mash-up, mostly grandkids.

"There are lives I can imagine without children," Mom read, "But none of them have the same laughter and noise."

This wasn't Dad's first look at this book. When it arrived a month or so before, I had shared it with Mom and Dad because I was excited about it. Among the many mixed blessings of Alzheimer's disease: I could share a gift once, and then bring it back a month later. Either Dad would see it as new or he would welcome it as familiar— a win either way. Dad did seem to recognize his grandkids in the photos. As mom helped him turn the pages, he grinned with the pride of a guy who has just caught a fly ball to end a big game; the guy who holds up his prize for all to see because he cannot believe his dumb luck.

"Now yours," I told Mom. Mom's gift was jammed into a white plastic garbage bag knotted at the top and adorned with only a red twist tie. I should have wrapped it. She would have liked it wrapped. She didn't say so, though. Lindy and I helped her tear the plastic bag away from the gift, a quilt, which we spread out over the bed, over Dad. Dad was alert, engaged, more as a spectator than a participant. He seemed so relaxed, like he was just along for this ride. He was always crazy about Christmas.

As the winter daylight worked its way through the window, warming the quilt, Lindy, Mom, and I stroked the its softly forgiving fabric, marveling at the intricate stitching, the blend of deep, earthy hues, the magic of a technology that could imprint a photograph of a sailboat onto fabric. We commented on the painstaking care someone had taken to create this unique and extraordinary, beautiful blanket.

Casually, Lindy looked up from our conversation and smiled, first at Dad and then at Mom and me. Dad's attention was on Lindy, whose round blue eyes always flash a distinctive glimmer whenever she's about to say something uncouth. No doubt, Dad caught it.

"Well, Dad," Lindy declared with a grin, "We could bore you to death!"

Part IV

Winter Birds

About Dying

We untie ourselves
Without knowing

Actively Dying

For a Moment

For a moment
When I sink into the knowing
I feel you breathe with His breath
The wind lifting ribbons
We untie ourselves without knowing
I like to hold you passing through
The ribbons gently waving on
The palm of my hand joining
Our passing on
One to another
A moment never changes
When you touch it that way

-        Penny

We are coming to the hard part of the story. Now, we know what's coming, but we wish not to know. Dad is not, at this stage, actively dying. Actively Dying is when the physical signs of death become very apparent. Actively Dying announces itself in different ways with every person, but generally involves dramatic changes in breathing, noticeable gurgling sounds, a decrease in responsiveness, and an increased—even extreme—agitation, sometimes referred to as fidgeting. The nurse wants to know, is he fidgety?

Fidgety. Hard to describe. Hard to watch. Fidgety is hard to understand before you've seen it. But after you've witnessed a dying person picking at bedclothes, reaching desperately into the distance, grabbing at people near the bed, calling for mama, sobbing, if you have used the word "fidgety" before, you will never use it the same way again.

After some mud wrestling with my conscience, I stepped out of the hospice picture for a weekend, in order to reconnect with my own family. Or so I thought. .My husband, whose name happens to be Jack, and I arrived at Cobo Center in time to honor Corporate Amerca's tradition of enjoying, two weeks before Christmas, a gala that is decidedly secular. As we stepped across the salted sidewalk, a punishing Michigan wind bullied us toward a wall of glass doors. My mind was full and my heart was heavy. I had too much to carry. Just as I realized this, Jack realized he had left our admission tickets in the car. He flagged down the valet making a turnaround in our Cadillac and gave me an opportunity to lighten up.

"I'm traveling light," I announced, tossing my purse into the trunk and handing Jack my lipstick and cell phone. Jack is familiar with cosmetics and cell phones. I am always doing this to him. Do other men carry pockets full of feminine necessities into social events? The TV show *Let's Make a Deal* should stage an episode at a corporate holiday ball. Jack would win every time.

   Inside the arena, we were greeted warmly by high-heeled hostesses and led into a swanky, carpeted ballroom, generously decked out for celebration. A patchwork of stylish people dotted the room, sewn together by beautiful servers carrying edible elegance on silver trays. A wall of windows lined the perimeter, framing the brilliance of the moonlight and a city outside whose sparkle could be rivaled only by the jewelry inside. This was Casino Night. People were here to party.

I Want to Travel Light

I want to travel light
Because my heart is so heavy
I pass a lipstick and a smart phone to
Mr. Used-to-This, who slips the weighty contraband
Into the right side pocket of his holiday sport coat
Traveling light means letting someone else carry something

We are gathered around a high table
Sharing drinks, laughing, when the smart phone
Begins its shiver
He reaches into his pocket, passes the grenade
Into my trembling hand

Each text an excruciating test
I step away from the gala, to the window wall,
Glance across the onyx river to
Where a city blinks to life
Text: Daughter wants takeout

My husband's eyes go wide, asking
My head shakes, no, in response
The phone drops into his pocket
He brushes crumbs of something
Away from his pressed white shirt

Again and again, I gaze across the sinister river
To the Milky Way that is Windsor,
Canada, right there, so foreign, so close
Traveling light means someone else shoulders the load

Son checks in. Sherpa's eyes ask; I shrug to say, not yet
Here, a photo: Dad in the La-Z-Boy, grinning
Daughter again: pizza man pulled over by police
I type: Tip Xtra
My courier, curious, returns a smile

We are watching our dealer's hands shuffle blackjack
when the phone shudders with a single word: Fidgety
Now sorrow boils up behind my closed eyes
Fidgety I comprehend
Fidgety crushes my tight heart into a protestor's fist
It is hands around my throat,
It is claws in both eyes
His eyes ask Mine answer
The vile object disappears again
Traveling light means unequally yoked

My sidekick tugs loose his festive noose
tosses a fistful of coins on the table
I want to travel light
My heart is just so heavy

-          Julie

Dad was "fidgeting." That was the word Mickey used but it seemed to her to be almost too passive to describe the agitated reaching motions that were coming in waves.

I had tried to warn them, tried to explain this part of the process to my siblings. When the nurse had asked, "Is he fidgeting?" they all nodded and said, yes, yes. I remember thinking, You pick your battles, and I pick this one. I spoke the nurse's name, firmly, just above a whisper; the voice that attracts curious children and quiets most adults. I looked into her eyes and said, "No, not yet."

My siblings were quiet then, and they let the nurse explain what was coming. But hearing and experiencing are two different ways of learning, so when it happened, they understood but were also surprised. I was sorry I wasn't there, with them, then. I had wanted to be there for that hard part. I had wanted to help with that.

Later, when asking others about their end-of-life experiences, Mickey would ask about "that thing," and, she said, people seemed to know what she meant. "Did your mom do that thing at the end? How long did it last? What did you do?"

"Here is what *we* did," said Mickey.

Mom, Mary, Penny, and I surrounded Dad, each in our position, waiting for the next wave. His brow would furrow, so slightly, then gradually the "thing" would begin, arms and legs rising and falling, reaching and clutching. Moans, cries, fear. An unwelcome roller-coaster ride, yet also familiar. During a lull, someone muttered, "Like labor."

We soothed as well as we could from our posts. We strained to match his anxious thrashing with all of the gentle serenity we did not feel inside. Our shhh's and slow motion hand strokes were the same hopeful motions we'd learned so long ago during those does-this-baby-have-colic-won't-sleep-tummy-ache nights.

We were rocking, swaying, calling on all our maternal comfort tools. Can we calm him this way? Can we move him through this? Can we make it stop? And then, please, God, make it stop. Later we talked about how hard it was, how sacred it was, how glad we were that it was us.

- Mickey

During one of the lulls, Mickey located the stack of neon stickers with the hospice phone number on them and radioed for backup. She told the nurse, "We gave him (drug one) and now he is agitated. He is really having a hard time."

Our hospice nurse, Jan, said, "You need to give him more drug one."

Mickey swallowed hard and explained, "I want to trust you. We gave my dad some drug one, and shortly afterward he started these motions that are really hard to watch. It looks like a seizure. He seems to be in a lot of pain. Now you are saying give him more?"

Nurse Jan responded, "Yes, and also, you want to give him drug two."

Mickey wasn't convinced, "In the Care Kit, we have a note, written in capital letters, saying not to give him that."

Nurse Jan was patient, "Give him x amount of drug one, and I am on my way."

Those were magic words. Mickey relayed Nurse Jan's message to the labor crew and they trusted her trust in Jan. They gave Dad some more of drug one and waited for the angel to arrive.

Sometime during this situation other angels arrived: Chris and Cliff. From the East and West Coasts, respectively, these two had caught the best flights available and touched down at Minneapolis-St. Paul International Airport within ten minutes of one another. Together, they took over the guest suite at River Village. They had each forfeited most creature comforts (spouses, sleep, decent meals) to be at Dad's side 24/7. Two or three days of that was enough for them, and for those around them. They were cajoled out the door and promised reentry only after a period of time equal to that of a feature-length film. They left with plans to see *The Hobbit*. Right in the middle of Dad's netherworld experience, they returned, wearing, of all things, Hobbit T-shirts.

"I almost bought the Hobbit footsy pajamas," said Chris, "but the laugh was not worth fifty dollars." Now, Chris, in his Hobbit T-shirt, leaned over Dad, held his hand right through a wave of flailing and wailing, and murmured words to comfort him. The sight of Chris in that shirt might have been enough to send Dad on the roller-coaster ride again, if he had noticed it. Let's just say a Hobbit T-shirt is not part of Chris' usual costume.

When the door opened next, it was Nurse Jan. She administered drug two and then invited everyone to join her in the living room.

She said, "This is it. He won't wake up now, but he can hear you and you can still give him the comfort and love you have been providing thus far. If you see two vertical wrinkles in his forehead, a number eleven, you can give him pain meds sooner than scheduled. This is about comfort now. You did a good job. You are all doing such a good job."

Nurse Jan was our angel that night. Traveling light requires bands of others: Sherpas, angels... they are used to this.

Palliative
A Vocabulary Lesson

"This is what's going to kill me." These are the words Dad muttered as people attempted clumsily to lift and move him from his bed to the bathroom and back. Does it hurt to die? People who know say, usually, yes. As the body shuts down, a dying person might experience discomforts ranging from numbness to general malaise to shooting pain. During the dying process, emotional and spiritual stress can compound the physical symptoms, adding to the physical discomfort.

The deeper Dad traveled into his cancer, the more acute his awareness and his ability to express himself seemed to be. We all noticed it; it was as if someone had pulled back the Alzheimer's Curtain and let the sun shine in. Perhaps the cure to Alzheimer's disease is hidden inside a cancer cell.

Dad said, "This is what's going to kill me." To the nonpsychologists among us, these seemed to be the words of a person with awareness of now and of the future. He had, on one page in his brain, the realization that he was going to die, and that it was this and not that which would claim him. These were the words of a person who could see the whole map, understand the destination, and declare that he would be taking a new and displeasing route through the forest. After Dad had lived with Alzheimer's disease for several years, the sudden clarity was a blessing, an unexpected gift. Dad was still in there, still with us.

Dad's awareness deepened my own frustration when I saw him in pain, especially when his discomfort was preventable.

"He is a nonambulatory patient," I scolded. The rage in my tone and the words I spat outvoice surprised everyone in the room and startled me, both because I meant what I saidthose words I'd spit out, and because I had never used the word, "nonambulatory," before. Later, I barked at Mary, "I do not ever want to see that again, not with Dad or anyone."

"But his dignity!" protested Mary, who had not seen the latest absurdity.

"Dignity? Do you think three people dragging Dad to a standing position and holding him off the ground to urinate is dignified? There is no dignity in that." I had been there. I had seen it. It was my ear he hissed into when the pain was too much. "This is what's going to kill me."

After that, he stayed in bed. The boys picked up a clear plastic container at Walgreens especially designed to accommodate a man's personal relief, which was used once or twice. But eventually, fluids became a nonfactor, so there was little output anyway. A day or two before he died, Nurse Jan catheterized Dad, and that part of the dignity conversation was over. Not to say the container didn't come in handy.

Lindy:	Rob, tell Ann this hotdish was amazing.
Rob:	Is there any left?
Lindy:	Just a little. I want to take some home to Vern but I can't find anything to put it in.
Penny:	Here you go! *(Tosses plastic urinal to Lindy.)*

The people moving Dad that time were not trying to hurt him. They could not have known how difficult it would be for him; they knew he was stubborn, insisting that he be allowed to do things the way he always had, even if his body refused to comply. We all did what we thought was right, until it became time to try something else. During hospice, the right gesture today sometimes becomes acan become don't-even-think-about-it activity within a day or two. Nonambulatory is another stage of loving.

Our dad, who in his twenties memorized the dictionary, would have been pleased to know about our expanding vocabulary. The word *palliative* crept in and stuck. Palliative. Now that's a word that rolls off the tongue. Palliative means soothing, or alleviating pain.

The ability of human beings to comfort one another is as old as pain itself. Thanks to ancient traditions and modern advancements in the study of palliative care, a dying person does not have to suffer extreme pain; most people can remain awake and involved in the world until the end. The objective is to manage pain appropriately, both through medication and also through the kind of comfort care that medicine can't compete with. Think about the ordinary gestures and diversions that bring anybody relief, and then offer these to your loved one.

The key is to watch for slight signals: a sigh or a smile means "Thank you." Any flinch, frown, or grimace means "Not now, please."

Bitter Pill

When our friends Eric and Jen were expecting their first child, they dutifully invested several Saturday mornings learning all there is to know about Lamaze and labor and lactating. My husband and I were in the same class, crowded with a dozen other couples into a steamy conference room adjacent to a hospital cafeteriathey. We rehearsed poses and inhaled deeply the aroma of the day's lunch preparations. TheyWe experimented with back massage and tennis balls, and imagined the ways a bathtub might come into play during life's inaugural event. Eric and Jen participated as directed. That is, until Eric had a problem.

You see, the course instructor, young and graceful, with tight little jeans and tight little hips that screamed, "I adopted mine," was describing labor, saying there are so many ways to comfort the laboring mother that "medication," she exclaimed, "is wholly unnecessary!"

That's when Eric lost it. He jumped out of his chair and shouted, "Are you kidding me?" The question might have included several expletives, but Eric self-censored. The expectants looked up, woke up, startled. Inside their mothers, babies began to kick and swim in response to the wild rumpus.

"No medicine?" demanded Eric. "Do you know what labor feels like?" The crowd looked curiously at the gentleman asking the question. Did he know? Yes, actually, he did know. By profession, Eric was a medical doctor working in obstetrics and gynecology. He knew. He knew all about comfort care. He knew that comfort care made all labors better. And he knew firsthand that, for some laboring mothers, there comes a time when all the comfort care in the world will not take the edge off. There comes a time when, exhausted, a woman's ability to "suck it up" and push runs out, causing unnecessary stress to her unborn child. Pain is different for everyone, during birth and death both.

What Eric knew for sure was that sometimes there is pain, and for that there are meds, and no person should be made to feel guilty for accepting what they need. As Eric put it, "You would not ask these women to have a tooth pulled without Novocain."

Eric's position was not that all birthing mothers should be put under; instead, reasonable care should be taken to keep the mother as involved and in tune as possible while relieving the pain that can create difficulties for herself and those around her, including her unborn sweet pea.

Every poet has a line or two comparing the mirror events that are our coming into and our leaving of life. There's a reason they do that. So, if birth and death are not really so far apart, then it's good to remember that, in both cases, there are many kinds of comfort. Knowing what is available to you and your loved one can make all the difference between a difficult birth/death and a beautiful, peaceful first/last breath.

Hospice professionals, who have seen all kinds of death scenarios, advise against waiting until pain is apparent. Start offering appropriate comfort medication early, before pain goes over the top. When medication is necessary, people know it. Pain looks like a mask distorting the familiar face of your loved one. A moment comes when caregivers look at one another and ask, "Isn't there something more we can do?" They wonder, "Another cold washcloth? Is that going to be enough this time?" That's when they remember the Care Kit.

The Care Kit is the package that the hospice team promised to deliver, and that they promised we would need.

It contained all the medications necessary to relieve the sudden onset of pain. No one thinks about it until they need it—and like a toothache needs a dentist, when the Care Kit is needed, it is definitely needed. So, when the time came, we called down to the nurse's station and requested the Care Kit be brought up. When no one delivered it, we called again and learned that is was gone. Gone? Gone.

Eventually, when it was recovered, Lindy took the lead on managing medications, but every one of us served time with the locked medicine box, its miniature key safely tied to a silver chain hanging from a cuckoo clock. We filled syringes, logged times and doses, and administered medications. The most pressing question, and it came up repeatedly as Team Lindy duked it out with anyone who crossed Dad, was this: Who advocates for people who don't have ten kids fighting their battles? Who advocates for the ghost lady down the hall when her time to go arrives? Are people left to fend for themselves?

Are you curious about where the Care Kit disappeared to? It's an interesting story, but, unfortunately, not an unusual story. What happens when someone's ethical boundaries stop right at the gates of hospice? What if someone believes the dying person should be allowed to live, to have the surgery, to eat and drink and dance? What if someone creates obstacles to good care? What if that person is in charge? What then? Well, Lindy and Penny found out firsthand.

It started innocently enough. At the intake meeting, our social worker and hospice nurse were clear about the needs Dad would have during his dying process.

The following Monday morning, a handful of us siblings were in the apartment at River Village when the social worker brought up the Care Kit, which had been delivered to the front desk.

"Here it is," the social worker showed us an innocuous bag of containers. She held it out, I suppose expecting one of us would take it. I'm sure she had had this conversation hundreds of times before; we had not. We looked at the package and at each other.

"I'll show you what's in here," she said. We watched her as if she were a model on QVC, pedaling jewelry or cleaning products. We did not want that package. Did it represent the end? No, we never thought about it that deeply. We did not have to. By nature, this family has a great sense of adventure; we also have a penchant for asking, "What can possibly go wrong?"

"There are some serious meds in there," someone remarked.

"Wouldn't want Virginia getting into those," someone agreed.

"Maybe there's a way to lock them up?" We asked the social worker to take the package downstairs to the nurse's station, where the meds could be locked up but easily accessed when the time came to dig into it. There is protocol, we said to ourselves. There are procedures, we told each other, nodding thoughtfully. It seemed like a good idea at the time. We saw the social worker again later the same day. It would be a long time before we would see the Care Kit again.

When Dad's pain was so intense that it could only be treated medically, those present knew it, without question and with no dissent. But when that time came, it did not happen to be during business hours; the nurses at River Village had, of course, gone home. To access the serious meds, understandably, the facility nurse on call had to connect with the hospice nurse and understand the situation. She would then contact an aide on site, who would unlock Oz and return to us what had been ours all along, our Care Kit. The family members on duty called hospice and then called the on-call facility nurse, Jill. Then the family waited patiently, practicing every palliative trick in the book, counting on Jill to stop the roller coaster of Dad's pain.

Five minutes. Fifteen. Thirty. Penny called hospice again, as Dad cringed in the bed beside her. No, they hadn't heard from Jill. Penny dialed Jill again to verify that she had the right number.

Jill answered, advising Penny, "Your mom shouldn't be administering these medications. You know, your father could have the surgery. My brother had the surgery. He's forty and completely healed now." Jill was generous with her medical advice. Penny was generous with her tact.

"Okay, well, my father is dying and he is in pain, and so he needs his medication." Penny was determined. She helped Jill along the wayas only a mother of four can help a person appreciate something. She continued, ingratiatingly, "So, you just call that number and leave a message; they will return your call."

"Oh, yes," said Jill. "I have called, but they haven't called back."

Penny was not buying that. Remember, she did raise four clever teenagers. Her collaborative attitude morphed into something cynical. "I spoke to the hospice nurse. She has not heard from you. My father is dying. He is in pain and he needs his medication. I am going to hang up now, just in case that nurse is trying to call you." Soon, an aide appeared with the coveted pills.

When challenged by a thorny task, people might naturally be inclined to defer to those with more experience. Penny and Linda did have some experience caring for people. Through high school, they worked together at Innsbruck, a nursing home, as Personal Care Attendants. During Dad's hospice, everyone knew their tacit role. As a family member, someone representing the patient, Penny thought she should let the paid medical professional in the room, an aide, dispense the medication. The aide declined, saying that was not within the scope of her responsibility. Finally, he agreed, but it was immediately clear that the aide truly did not know how to dispense medicine.

"He wanted to give him the pill to swallow with a glass of water." Penny was still alarmed days later when she recounted the story for those of us who were not there at the time.

"I said, 'No, no, no. It goes under the tongue!'"

There is a right way to do some things, which is easy to learn. While they had been waiting for the Care Kit to appear, the hospice nurse had explained to Penny exactly what to do when it arrived.

"There's a little blue pill," the nurse explained. "This is all you have to do—you can do this—just put it under his tongue."

And so, in the end, she did.

The aide was right to set a boundary where it belonged. Jill, however, threw up more than a few unnecessary hurdles between Dad and his medications. One morning, Jill knocked on the door and announced, in her grave and cavernous voice, "I have to talk to the family." Lady, if you're here, you're family. Start talking.

She wanted to know why the family needed so much medication. Everyone pointed at Lindy, who had been up all night knowing exactly why we needed more medication. It wasn't for Dad. It was, but it wasn't.

"What happened," said Lindy, later, "was that when she didn't bring Dad's medications a second time and then a third time, I called and requested a new prescription. But she kept asking why we needed more. It was like she was saying we took it."

The day Jill confronted Lindy, Lindy was matter-of-fact, saying, "We have a right to administer this medication and I want it all. We'll lock it up, we'll keep a chart for you, whatever you want, but we want it."

It wasn't the hospice organization interfering; it wasn't River Village, either. It was one person who had a weighty ethical belief that the ninety-year-old man drifting in and out of consciousness on the big bed might somehow pull a Lazarus and start skipping rope or playing the saxophone. Jill had been informed of Dad's prognosis, that he had just these few days left to live, but she didn't believe it.

Jill knew Dad only casually. She worked as a nurse in an assisted-living facility; he lived there for a few years, receiving his assistance almost entirely from his wife and requiring little, if any, skilled nursing care during that time. The aides knew him well and went out of their way to comfort and assist him; his kids knew him well; his wife, well, she knew him pretty well, too. And yet, it was this near stranger who felt compelled to judge the decisions being made.

The night Dad died, Lindy ran into Jill sitting in the stairwell, the family's secret shortcut between Mom and Dad's apartment and the Boys' Room downstairs. The rebel was "bawling her eyes out," according to Lindy, who doesn't exaggerate. Jill had finally been hit over the head with the realization that people die sometimes.

Lindy was trapped. Jill looked up from her seat on the middle step and spilled out an apology that echoed in the stairwell. "I'm so sorry," she wailed. "I didn't know. I did not know. I had no idea." Bawling her eyes out.

Lindy just stared at her, thinking, "We told you." Her next thought was, "Are you a nurse? Or maybe not?"

"Did you say that?" I asked Lindy later.

"Of course not, but I thought it." She went on, "I do believe Jill had a change of heart that night. But it wasn't much help to us."

We were told that Dad's death was the first hospice event at River Village, which introduced a variety of riddles into the mix. For example, the kitchen staff, bless them, were required to follow food service protocol even when doing so was wasteful and made no sense at all to anyone. River Village provides quality care for the living. Therefore, the staff is obligated to provide meals to its residents.

And Dad was a resident. We said, "No, thank you," and then, "Thank you." After a while, we simply ignored the trays of food coming and going at regular intervals: meatloaf, chicken soup, and lasagna, all for a man in a bed who could not sit up, let alone swallow. Dad had always enjoyed meals in the Village dining room—he delighted in conversing with the staff and other residents, he appreciated the flowers on the tables, and he relished the occasional ice cream bar for dessert. But during these last few days of his life, he had already been excused from the table.

My dad would want you to know, there were others. Accommodating staff members went out of their way to care for our family. Jill's supervisor, when she caught wind of the medication situation, came to the door loaded down with everything—every medication prescribed to our father.

"These are yours," she told Lindy.

Later, we learned that, thanks to her experience with our dad, this leader initiated hospice training for her staff. Until Dad's hospice experience, they had no protocol for allowing residents to die at home. So, here comes our Dad, the pioneer, pioneering again.

Night Shifts

True love causes pain. Jesus, in order to give us
the proof of his love, died on the cross. A
mother, in order to give birth to her baby, has
to suffer. If you really love one another, you will
not be able to avoid making sacrifices.

- Mother Teresa

Overnight shifts are tough. Adults who are accustomed
to working by day and falling asleep during *The Late Show
Starring Jimmy Fallon* are not quick adapters to shift work. They
forget to nap during the day, and they come back at night more
tired than ever. Their hearts are worried, their minds are full,
and they are wearing the wrong clothes: jeans instead of
sweatpants. They are eating the wrong foods, more junk, no
schedule; maybe they are not eating at all. It makes for thin
skins and delicate nerves. It makes for arguments so intense
that, often, sibling relationships die right along with the parent
the siblings are there to care for. It doesn't have to happen that
way, but it can.

Flashback: Night Shift at the Heart Hospital

When Dad was eighty-four years old, doctors agreed that
the man whose heart was beating at 23 percent of normal was
otherwise healthy. Healthy enough to be plugged in and
recharged, and this optimistic medical team proceeded to
open up our dad and insert a medical device that would
eventually manage 100 percent of his heartbeats while he

enjoyed life with his wife, his grandchildren, his golf buddies. Without that pacemaker, Dad would have wound down like a train whistle fading in the distance. Without that mini-miracle, he would not have had five more years to live a full and satisfying life. However, the troll under the bridge crossing from 23 percent to the greener pastures of "five more years" was a little one named Hospital Stay.

Following surgery, thinking he would be better off, the medical staff at the hospital sent home the ten adult children and their mother who had gathered in the ICU waiting room. By midnight, the forced separation untethered Dad's true colors: the hospital staff surrendered to the truth that Dad was best off when surrounded by his People.

Lindy had never actually left the premises; she was camped out in a nearby lobby when the night nurses called for backup. It was agreed that Mom should stay home and sleep, so a few kids signed on to split the night shift. Penny and I took the 2 am to 10 am stretch, and spent most of that early morning keeping Dad in his bed by talking with him about whatever was on his mind. He wanted to go home. He wanted to see his wife.

"What kind of place," he asked us, "doesn't let you call your wife when you want to?"

There are people in the medical profession who believe that hospitals bring out the dementia in otherwise sharp senior citizens. Our dad's first indication of dementia was a case in point. It was documented on a medical chart the morning someone woke up Dad in his ICU suite and declared it. The nurse entered the darkened room and roused Dad, subsequently rousing Penny and me, as well. We had been snoozing more or less comfortably in straight-backed plastic chairs on either side of Dad's bed.

The nurse asked Dad his name, twice. Dad would have rubbed his eyes and tried to focus, but his hands were strapped to boards with IVs attached. He came around and stated his name: Jack I. Moore. Then the nurse asked Dad for the date. The man who had been asleep a moment before, and under general anesthesia the day before and who had been awakened throughout the night for critical care such as blood pressure readings and alarms going off, the man whose watch had been removed and who didn't have a calendar on the wall or a newspaper to refer to, that man looked toward the slit of daylight sneaking through closed curtains, perhaps to gauge how much time had passed since he last stood outside in the sun. Then he turned to his middle-aged daughters, who watched him with interest. You see, this is the kind of moment in which Dad would typically make a wisecrack. Instead, he surrendered. "I don't know," he said.

The nurse wrote "Dementia" in bubble letters with stars and frowning faces all around it and left the room with the result she had been expecting. When she was gone, Dad stared up at the ceiling. Having already lost track of days and nights myself, I asked Penny, "Do you know today's date?"

"Nope."

Dad didn't comment, but when he heard us chuckling, he did crack a smile.

Later that day, after a good rest, I took Dad for a wheelchair ride around the hospital. After traveling the long, gleaming white tiled corridors in left turns for a half hour or so, Dad started backseat driving. "Turn right," he demanded, more than once.

"Dad, we can't turn right. That's the exit."

"I know! Let's get out of here!"

Jay Takes a Night Shift

After someone dies, it can be comforting to those who go on living to believe their loved one is still connected to them somehow. That they are "watching over us" or manipulating situations in our favor, while taking breaks from their afterlife of singing angel carols and reclining on the clouds. Our brother Jay shows up in our lives from time to time. Always the joker, it is never a surprise when he plays a prank. Throughout our adult lives, we have exchanged Jay stories. We all have a few.

If ghosts and angels exist, it seems perfectly reasonable that, in the days leading up to Dad's death, Jay would be hanging out in the hospice apartment at River Village. We like the idea of Jay being a part of our lives, even now, and we appreciate that he was not in too much of a hurry to escort Dad to his heavenly home. Jay was up late the night Penny was in charge.

Penny wanted her night shifts to be tranquil. Someone remarked that Dad would soon have plenty of time to catch up on his rest; Penny didn't see the humor in that, if there was any. She stationed herself next to Dad's bed and trekked out to the living room every four seconds to tell Lindy and Mom and me to stop talking.

"You must go outside if you need to talk out loud," she admonished us children in her smoky whisper. She was pointing toward the door, in case we were confused about the location of the apartment's only exit. Mom surrendered and crawled into bed beside Dad. Lindy and I kept talking, thinking we were whispering, although we were probably shouting. Suddenly, Penny emerged through the bedroom doorway, hollering in pantomime, both arms akimbo, her hair standing on end.

She gestured wildly for a minute, threw up her silent hands, and stomped back into the darkened room. We stifled our giggles. Teenagers at a sleepover, up way too late.

"Why didn't she just say be quiet?" Lindy wondered. More giggles. But we knew Penny's request was reasonable, and it wasn't Lindy's shift anyway, so she decided to leave.

Lindy and I were now in the far corner of the living room. Far, far from the piano. The piano. Whose cover—BAM!—slammed shut just at that moment, who threw its music, folders, photos, and papers violently across the floor. We were nowhere near it. When Penny burst through the doorway again, we both raised our open hands in the air, as if we were under arrest, or as if to say, "Hey! Wasn't us!"

We leaped forward in the dark to pick up the papers and I murmured to Lindy, "This has to be a message from someone. Look for a sign." As I said it, she pointed out the only piece of paper facing up; the rest were facedown. It was a photo of Jay.

"Jay!" Lindy exclaimed. She shook her index finger at the photo as if the joker were in the room beside her, because he probably was.

The next morning, Chris said he wasn't surprised by Jay's trick at all. He said, "Jay does stuff like that to me all the time." Recalling one incident, his bright blue eyes literally twinkled—I saw the flash. He described a Florida vacation day at a zoo with his family. They were appreciating a crowded blue jay exhibit. Chris was quietly admiring the birds and thinking affectionate thoughts of Jay when all of a sudden, splat, one of those feathered friends pooped right on his shoulder. Jay!

You Are Not God

When words cut glass, elephant hearts are only hiding.

-        Rob

Night shifts exact a high physical and emotional toll from caregivers. People need sleep. The fallout of every night shift is visible every morning after; the battle wounds of worry, exhaustion, and lack of creature comforts wear a person thin. The night shifts with Dad were tough not because they went on awhile, but because we were so afraid there would not be many more. It was sunup after one of those nights, while Chris and I were measuring medicine into syringes and scraping dried mounds of orange sherbet off the kitchen counter, that our conversation turned from quiet to careless.

Chris and I are close in age and, I think, close in spirit. I admire Chris and he is a good friend to my family. Chris' loyalty runs deep. That I would jeopardize that, well, it still saddens me. One chippy little comment, tossed out there, and Chris was infuriated. At me, and my big mouth.

"You are not God." Chris spat those words, one at a time, into the stale morning air of the claustrophobic kitchen. You. Are. Not. God.

He was right, of course. If any one of us were God, would we be standing in that kitchen that morning, on the Memory floor, crushing morphine pills with the back of a spoon? If any one of us were God, would we not have stopped this circus, cured Dad's cancer, and moved on? Would we not be on a beach or in a theater or at home with our own children, if one of us were God?

What I had said to set him off was, "It is today."

I did not say, "I hope it's today," or "Put your money on lights out by 9:00." But I also did not say, "I wonder if…" or "I hope not, but…" or "I have a feeling…" I spoke too fast, too bluntly. I said words that came out gnashing their terrible teeth, roaring a terrible roar. I forgot gentleness and empathy. I forgot how hard we all were hoping that it wouldn't be today. I forgot to not give up. I forgot how tired we both were. I blurted. And he spat, "You. Are. Not. God." But where was God just then, anyway? Maybe God was downstairs, waiting, because he knew, as sure as hot air and tempers would rise, our arguments would descend to the Boys' Room.

Our communication intensity meter peaked just a few days before Dad's death. We went into this situation pretty much as friends. We were ten siblings, varying in appearance and personality about as much as any random ten people on the planet, but we genuinely liked enough traits about one another that, to a one, we would say we were friends. And to a one, we shared a single motivation: help Mom to help Dad.

So, you take ten friends. Lure them into a room with four chairs and no Internet. Bring a gentleman into the room. In a bed. Tell them the gentleman is going to die while they are in the room. Tell them that if the man cries out in fear or pain, only they can relieve him.

Feed the chums coffee, diet pop, hot dish, and pheasant pie. Send in strangers: someone wearing a high-necked nightgown, someone walking at a slant, as if her personal earth were the top deck of the Titanic, just before it sank. Send in a long-lost cousin. Send in someone carrying medicines that they know will cause the gentleman nausea and delirium. Send in a ghost. Forbid loud voices, ringers on phones, and laughter after dark. Forbid the people to disagree in front of the gentleman. Force them to stay awake.

Tell them this will last two to four days. Leave them there for five, then six. Return after a week, and, with a wide, toothy smirk, rub your twisted, bony hands together and ask, "How is everyone getting along?" It can't possibly end well.

Ask around. Siblings from all classes of families will admit that some of them don't speak to one another. We once stayed with a family on a week-long summer vacation in a seven-bedroom home and only on day four discovered that some of the adults in the host family did not speak to one another. Ever. If you hate people, it is actually easier to ignore each other in a crowd. The week before Dad's death, a family friend lost her mother. Because of disagreements about caring for mom, the siblings were all so bitter that they forbade one family member to attend the mother's funeral. Our family would not be going there.

Instead, we went to the first-floor apartment, Chris and Cliff's rented villa, which had become the Boys' Room. There was no Girls' Room. The Boys' Room was always unlocked and everyone used it to nap or shower or brush teeth when they thought of it. The room was also used as a place to vent.

That morning, I followed Chris down the back staircase to the Boys' Room. He sat on the bed and I sat across from him on the couch. I uncrossed my arms and leaned forward. He looked away. Then he turned back to me and said a few things. I said a few things.

One thing I said, which was difficult to say, was, "If I don't tell you this now, I will never speak to you when this is over, and that is not what I want." He glared. I deserved it.

A few siblings piped in. Clearing the air is messy business. Words like bossy and angry and inattentive come out, along with other words: trust, care, listen. Under pressure, people develop tunnel vision, believing their way must be the best way. We were forgetting that we were all here for the same purpose. Which of us didn't love Dad? I apologized. He apologized. Or maybe he apologized first. It was over.

Or was it? Trust is a delicate thing. A Weeble, really. Isn't it "Weebles wobble but they don't fall down"? Once trust gets pushed, it starts to wobble, and it takes a while for it to stand solidly upright again. You can't really help it along. You just have to let it go, and avoid knocking it over again if you can. We had to be careful with each other.

The Boys' Room was a good place to say what we needed to say. There was some urgency to it, too, a need to keep things okay between us. We had too much to do to let anger simmer. We had to work it out.

Among Dad's last words, spoken the same day, were, "Protect family." Protect family? Perhaps he could hear us through the floorboards or the ductwork. He knew that to protect our relationships, we had to work at it. And he knew that we would try.

Dad did not die that day. So I was wrong, and Chris was right. There is a God, and we are not Him. But we lean on Him, and we are grateful for Him.

> **Now God be praised, that to believing souls**
> **Gives light in darkness, comfort in despair**
> **(2.1.64–65) Shakespeare, *Henry IV***

Protect Family

The best overnight shift is the one you share with lawyers. Lawyers crave order. And sleep. They draw up a task list and respect it.

✓ Greet the team.
✓ Assess strengths of all members. Who's tired? Who's wired?
✓ Do the math. Over a six-hour shift covered by three people, each person can sleep for four hours:

12a.m.–2a.m.	2 a.m.–4 a.m.	4 a.m.–6 a.m.
Brian awake	Julie awake	Terry awake
J and T asleep	B and T asleep	B and J asleep

✓ Set alarms on phones of all participants.
✓ Begin.

At two a.m., I stretched my kinked neck a couple of times, untangled myself from the double La-Z-Boy recliner, and told Brian, "I'm up." The apartment was shadowy, almost murky, everything distorted by a yellow light glowing over the stove. Nothing had changed. Dad's breathing was quiet, and the pauses between his breaths were extended.

"I think he's comfortable," whispered Brian. We discussed whether or not to wake him to dose out the next meds, and remembered that the nurse had said to administer this medicine, specifically, on schedule. It was quietly tucked in along Dad's cheek, and Brian went down to the Boys' Room to sleep. The bells on the door made a barely audible sigh as the door clicked closed and Brian's key turned in the lock from the outside.

I took his place, still warm, in the chair beside the bed, dozing, praying, listening, counting Dad's inhales and exhales, wondering about whether Mom was comfortable. In lieu of bringing a hospital bed into the crowded apartment, someone had had the creativity to prop up the old bed by placing pillows under the mattress at its head. This seemed to help keep Dad from choking, kind of kept the natural juices running down the back of his throat; we had meds for that, too, but did not use them much. The death rattle was never really a thing with Dad.

We had stuffed one or two pillows beneath the mattress on the side of the bed, too, so Dad would not roll off. All this ingenuity left very little room for Mom alongside him.

We called it the Big Bed, but it was not big. Big Bed referred to the king-sized bed our parents used while we were growing up. Sick children could sleep in the Big Bed. Grandchildren could watch TV on the Big Bed. When relatives came to celebrate Thanksgiving, everyone put their coats on the Big Bed. The bed Dad was dying in tonight did not seem big at all, and I wondered if Mom might be falling off the other side.

Suddenly, Mom sat straight up, which made me bolt straight up, too.

I whispered, "Mom, are you okay?"

Mom answered in her full, singsong, middle-of-the-day outside voice, "I've been thinking," she said. "When Chris was reading Dad's book today, the chapter about leaving for the war. I was thinking there were some similarities to what we're doing now."

"Like what?" I whispered.

"About leaving. Read it. Tell me what you think," blared Mom.

"Do you want me to read it aloud?"

"Sure."

I held my cell phone over the book for light and began to read softly.

"Wow, Mom. You're right."

Mom said, "I was thinking, we could read it at the wake or something." She was still using a voice that would certainly wake Terry, sleeping in the recliner in the living room, and would have irked some of my other siblings. However, for Mom, not waking Dad (or Terry) was not a concern.

"Maybe..." I didn't know how to tell her what the problem here might be.

"But it's too long," added Mom, which was what I had been thinking.

"Maybe I could edit it, just pull together the parts that relate," I offered. I had never given Dad as much time as he had needed and wanted to help him with his book; there was always something else to do. Now I had nothing *but* time. And yet, time was running out.

"I'll do it, Mom, but you need to go back to sleep. I'll wake you up when I'm done."

I found a notebook and downloaded a flashlight app to my phone. With one foot on the bed next to Dad's, I balanced his book, my notebook, and the phone and began to rewrite the chapter by hand. The setup was too complicated. I had to find a better way.

I could hear the even breathing of Mom sleeping now, and I hated to wake her. I tried flipping on the bathroom light, but if it was dim enough to let people sleep, it wasn't bright enough to write by.

Finally, I situated myself at the kitchen table, choosing an angle that allowed me to see by the light above the stove, but also to keep Dad in my line of vision. The arrangement reminded me of keeping watch over my children as they drifted off to sleep. Patrick, especially, had preferred to have someone in a chair in his room while he waited under his multisport fleece blanket for the sandman to come around. Now a young adult, Patrick wants nothing less in the world than a parent in his room, staring at him as he sleeps. Dad wouldn't be needing me much longer, either.

An hour flew by. Suddenly, Mom sat up again. "How's it coming?" She was instantly up and walking around.

I told her, "Mom, when you get back into bed, I will read this to you. It's really good."

These were Dad's words, Dad's description of what he was going through the morning he left for the army, a mirror of what he was going through now. His words said, "Leaving is not going to be easy," and "It pulls at my heart to say 'goodbye' instead of 'good night,'" and "She is in pain, and my leaving is the cause." These lines are part of the thing, but the other part, in the mirror, is a man who has to go, wants to go, yet feels the tug of his loved ones to stay, to keep things as they have been, to not cause pain to anyone.

I read my version to Mom, and she was pleased. I hoped Dad was listening, too. They say that the sense of hearing stays until the end, even after the other senses shut down; I was counting on it.

The next day, I explained to my brothers that Mom wanted to use this part of Dad's book at the wake or funeral. They read the condensed version and Chris flipped it back to me, saying, "Don't forget the last chapter."

Chris, who had invested more time than anyone helping Dad edit his book, knew exactly what was needed. In an instant, he whipped open the book to a section that began, "I have had my wakeup call." Amazing how quickly he found it, how certain he was about adding that on. It was the end of the war, and Dad was writing about going home.

It starts, "I have had my wakeup call. Today's target will be another world, safer but much less orderly than you and your friends have known in the last few years." No question: it was perfect. However, at that point, who could know how perfect, exactly? The section ends, "Briefing will be at 1950 hours this evening." When Dad died, the time was 1910 hours. Close enough. In Africa, it's said that America is five miles from heaven. Maybe they're right: a forty-minute walk, give or take a few.

Saying Goodbye

Dad's last communiqués were mostly loving and kind. When he had to be moved, which caused him a great deal of pain, he said, "This is what's going to kill me." But that was a statement of fact, not a reflection of his feelings for any of us. He had a few things he needed to share, and he fervently worked to do so. This effort was a profound gift to us, but sometimes a gift we were challenged to unwrap.

Mickey was in the bedroom with Dad, holding his hand one late afternoon as he stared out the window, one of his last days. As she described the conversation, Dad's voice was low, stretched thin by his age and debility.

He said, "I think this looks like a day I'd like to play golf."

Mickey agreed. "It's a perfect day to play golf."

After a bit, he said, "Do you know what I'd like to do?"

Mickey: What, Dad?

Dad: *(insert profound and important insights that Mickey couldn't hear or understand)*

Mickey: Yes, yes, I see.

Dad: *(looks Mickey straight in the eye)* Will YOU do that?

Mickey: *(gulps)* Of course. Yes.

Dad: Right away?

Mickey: Yes. *(Pauses)* How will I know if I did the right thing?

Dad: *(Gives Mickey that "duh" look, which can only be interpreted as, "Of COURSE you'll do the right thing and of COURSE you'll know.")*

Someone asked Mickey what Dad's greatest gift to her might have been. She thought of Optimism and of Possibility.

This moment was a great illustration of how Dad passed along his optimism. He saw possibilities in each person, and he believed people should follow their callings.

After Dad died, Mickey declared the next twelve months "The Year of 'What if I'm as good as my dad always said I am?'" At the end of the year, I asked her about it. She smiled her usual, knowingly confident smile.

"What I found out," she said, "is that I am."

Sharon's goodbye came one evening, at the end of a visit to the apartment.

> I was about to leave and Dad was in bed. He had been weak and was not communicating. I leaned over and kissed him and said, "Bye, Dad. Love you." He reached up, put his arms around me and kissed my cheek. I could feel his kiss and hear it. I will hold it in my heart forever.

Our faith tradition includes a sacrament called "Anointing of the Sick." Also referred to as "Last Rites," this ritual is a blessing for those going into surgery or who are very ill, as well as those who are dying. Traditionally, this is led by a church leader (priest, deacon), but there is no rule against lay people performing the blessing. Contrary to many people's understanding, a person can have "Last Rites" more than once. Dad received the sacrament at least a couple times during his lifetime.

When we explained Dad's status to Father Bill, he came over and performed the ritual, saying some prayers, crossing Dad's forehead with holy water, asking the heavens to accept him if and when it is their will to do so.

After the blessing, Father Bill, an old friend of Dad's, asked him what he would say the day he faced his Creator.

Dad did not miss a beat. "I will say, 'Oh, my God.' And I will mean it!"

In retrospect, it seems Dad knew well before we did that his life was coming to a close. We have a relative who lives in Mexico for several months every winter. In November, before Dad's cancer diagnosis, just before she left Minnesota, she made time to visit with him. He surprised her. Saying goodbye, he took her hand in both of his. He told her, "I won't see you again." They both had tears in their eyes. They both knew what that meant.

He said the same thing to his son-in-law Sergio on Thanksgiving Day, "I won't see you again." He and Sergio did see each other once again, but Dad was very ill by that time and unable to communicate clearly.

For another son-in-law, Vern, Dad's goodbye was the usual too-hearty handshake.

Vern said, "Take it easy, Jack."

Dad's response was just as casual, "See you in the next life." That was the Sunday before Dad died and it happened to be their last conversation.

Lindy, on the other hand, did not get off so lightly. Dad had a "responsibility" for her. When we were eleven kids under age thirteen, each older sibling had a younger one to look out for, to care for, to keep an eye on. It was a kind of buddy system within the family. I was Penny's 'sponsibility. Now, Dad had a responsibility in mind for Lindy. He told her, "Help me help them. You'll know." That's all Lindy needed to hear.

Very late in the game, Dad gathered his boys around him. Or, rather, the boys happened to gather. Mom was there, too, everyone straining to hear what Dad was trying to say. Chris, being the thinker in the group, came in bearing pen and legal pad, hoping to record Dad's message. Because of this, in spite of the problems posed by Dad's failing voice and medicated thought stream, there exists documentation in the form of a yellow legal pad covered in hieroglyphics. As best as anyone can tell, the essence of the moment was this, elucidated by Rob:

He had to go. He wondered about and was concerned for his wife and family.

I said, "We won't let you down," and he said, "That's the truth."

It seemed to me that he knew this was his opportunity to share some things that were really important to him. It was hard for him to speak, but he clearly had the intent of giving us a message or messages, and he noticed when we drew in closer to hear him. He wasn't fading in and out of consciousness or anything like that. He clearly had intent to speak to us and share his thoughts.

He looked at us and knew we were there. I believe he understood, and was very in touch with the moment. When Mom walked into the room, he gave an apologetic grin and said, "I'm sorry, sweetheart." That might have been the clearest thing he said.

I remember us asking, "Who do you see?" and I see that question in the notes, but I don't remember Dad's answer. Once, I remember his referencing "army" people standing by me when I was at the foot of the bed, but it was hard to be sure.

We know for sure that he said, "Protect the family," and I believe he said, "Protect Emily." He mentioned Mom's name several times; I know that. He had a hard time saying her name and he was very slow and deliberate when he pronounced it.

I think we can honor Dad's words by continuing to be there for each other and for Mom, and by making sure we never become strangers. We tried our best to hear everything Dad said, and I am grateful that Chris thought to take notes.

                                -        Rob

Winter Birds

When our brother Jay, nicknamed Bluejay, died on a winter evening at the age of eighteen, Rob wrote a poem about a blue jay alighting from time to time and staying just long enough to remind us that our Bluejay is with us, still.

Dad's grief over his son's untimely death was understandably profound. Shortly after Jay's death, Dad was heard saying, "Twenty years, just twenty years and I'll be with you again." It turned out to be thirty-seven years later, that prefigured December night, when Dad was called upon to play out the final lines of Rob's poem so that father and son could be together again.

Winter Birds

A Blue Jay sits atop the snow
Just long enough for us to know
Loved ones lost are always near
Somehow they always find us here

A certain flower, make of car
A train at night, or falling star
They shake us from our winter frost
Reminding us of loved ones lost

These little signs that come so far
Flash like moments where we are
Though we toil on our own
They tell us we are not alone

Here a moment, then away
We see them but they cannot stay
They sail into the winter sky
And we can only watch them fly

Years from now, December night
In memory's ever dimming light
Your thoughts will cast you back and then
You'll see the Blue Jay land again

See the colors, hear the song
This time it bids you come along
Follow close and you will know
Where all the winter Blue Jays go

Home at last, you both shall fly
When God alights the winter sky

-        Rob

They Will Ask You Questions and You Will Know the Answers

Let's Go

Let's go...
You walk with me
Hold my hand
Guide my way

You walk with me
I hold your arm, not too tight
How about a hug?

We walk
Bonded to our destination
Steering, supporting
Where are we going?
We will be there soon
How about a hug?

We walk, you ride
I am your legs
I am your direction
Together we go, we will get there
How about a hug?

I walk with
You on an angel's wings
We made it
I can feel you hugging me

-        Lindy

Death is a process, a transition. Many people who have witnessed the death of a loved one explain that they felt that the person was still present after their physical body had completely shut down. Others who witness the moment of death describe it with the words "gone" and "empty." There may be a sense of departing or a sense of finality. Either way, while caregivers may feel prepared for the process of death, people's reactions when it happens might be surprising. A chart or list posted prominently will help those present to remember what to do when the time comes.

Signs that death has occurred include no breathing, no heartbeat, release of bowel and bladder, eyelids slightly open, eyes fixed on a certain spot. When you have determined that death has occurred, what then?

Use the chart on the next page to guide your next steps. We taped this list on the side of Mom and Dad's refrigerator, and the people who were there when Dad died mentioned that they were glad it was there. You'll see there are two copies of the chart on the following pages. It's okay to rip one page out of this book, if you want, and tape it up where people can easily see it.

After the body has been removed, you may choose to spend time with loved ones, or you might want to be alone. Respect and care for yourself now. Even if others want your time or attention, let yourself process this loss in your own way, at your own pace.

A Hospice Death Is NOT a Medical Emergency
DO NOT call paramedics or emergency services.

If you do, they are required to respond
and they are required to attempt resuscitation.

This Is What You Need to Do:

What time is it? Write down the time of death or stop the hands of a clock to remind you later on.

Call hospice to inform them of the death. They will ask you some questions, and you will know the answers.

Take some time. It's okay to gently wipe away any bodily fluids that were released. Wash your loved one's face and comb his hair. Replace teeth and gently close his eyelids.

If his jaw has fallen open, you can try to close it. Keep it closed by propping his head up slightly and placing a rolled towel under his chin. If it doesn't stay closed, that's okay.

Call family members and close friends who need to be notified immediately. Others can be contacted later.

Complete any religious or personal rituals that are important to your loved one.

After everyone has said goodbye, call the funeral home where your arrangements were made. The people there will ask you a few questions, and you will know the answers.

A Hospice Death Is NOT a Medical Emergency
DO NOT call paramedics or emergency services.

If you do, they are required to respond
and they are required to attempt resuscitation.

This Is What You Need to Do:

What time is it? Write down the time of death or stop the hands of a clock to remind you later on.

Call hospice to inform them of the death. They will ask you some questions, and you will know the answers.

Take some time. It's okay to gently wipe away any bodily fluids that were released. Wash your loved one's face and comb his hair. Replace teeth and gently close his eyelids.

If his jaw has fallen open, you can try to close it. Keep it closed by propping his head up slightly and placing a rolled towel under his chin. If it doesn't stay closed, that's okay.

Call family members and close friends who need to be notified immediately. Others can be contacted later.

Complete any religious or personal rituals that are important to your loved one.

After everyone has said goodbye, call the funeral home where your arrangements were made. The people there will ask you a few questions, and you will know the answers.

Curtains of Night

He asked, What are you trying to do?
She said, I am kissing you.
He said, I love that.

We were not all there the moment Dad died. We were not all watching when our mother kissed our father, and he exhaled one last time.

Those on the upcoming night shift had ducked out for a rest. I went to find supper for my kids and see about homework. My son, Patrick, was out and about, but my girls were home. Their dad was traveling and I had been spending long hours at River Village, so the teens had passed the last few evenings solo.

Over a dinner of BLTs and carrots, I asked, "How has it been going?"

Maureen:	Fine
Kasey:	We're actually better without you.
Me:	?
Maureen:	(*nods*) We've been doing the dishes and getting up on time in the morning and not fighting at all.
Me:	So I should move into River Village and let you kids run the house?
Kasey:	Yep.
Me:	Until you run out of groceries.
Girls:	(*Teenage eye roll*)
Me:	I feel bad leaving you alone overnight, but I feel bad leaving Grandpa, too.
Girls:	Is he going to die soon?

Me:	I think so.
Girls:	You don't seem very sad.
Me:	*(Thinking about that)* I am sad, for myself. But would you deny him heaven?

Not all of us were there the moment Dad died. My mother took my father to the gates, kissed him once, and he was home. As it happened, Terry and Lindy and I were all at our homes, too, standing at the islands in each of our respective kitchens, talking with our children. Similar scenes must have played out in the same way at all three houses. Here's how it looked through the windows of the all-white kitchen where I stood at the island with Kasey and Maureen:

Ringing phone.

Me:	It's Mickey. *(Long pause and then, not Hello, not, What's up, just)* Is he gone?
Mickey:	Dad died. Just a minute ago. Nat King Cole was on the radio. It was really quiet and calm. Nice.
Me:	I'm on my way.

The sound a phone makes as it is placed gently on a kitchen counter can shatter silence, especially of the variety engulfing that kitchen.

Is he gone?

Nod. Cry. Hugs. Are you going to go there?

I want you to go there with me. Let's find Patrick.

What followed was fog. Calling my husband and oldest daughter, both out of town. Listening to "Solid Colors" on the way, and "Heavenly Day," and a few other songs because it took a lifetime to get there. Looking in from the doorway as the others read a blessing to Dad, feeling left out, lonely, so sad. Trying, needing, to close his mouth. Why? Who cares? Where are his teeth? Shouldn't his mouth be closed? Kissing his forehead. Again. And again. The look in the girls' eyes, their expressions mirrors of one another. Telling them, "You can touch him. You can touch his arm." Why? Why would I make them do that?

There is a scene in William Shakespeare's *Hamlet* when the conversation turns to death. Says Hamlet, "There is special providence in the fall of a sparrow. If it be now, 'tis not to come; if it be not to come, it will be now; if it be not now, yet it will come. The readiness is all."

Readiness? For death? Who is ever ready? When a person travels through hospice care, death is the ultimate destination. Intellectually, everyone knows this. Everyone thinks that, in the moment that death occurs, they will be ready. Everyone imagines they know how the scene will play out; they see it coming and they think they can predict their own reactions. And still, we surprise ourselves.

In the TV series "How I Met Your Mother," there's an episode called "Bad News" in which Marshall (played by Jason Segel) faces the death of his father. It's a memorable episode, with a poignant scene in which Marshall puts words around the feeling so many of us have when a loved one passes on. He says, "I'm not ready for this."

Grappling for language immediately after my own father's passing, the only words I found formed the same, simple declaration. I stood in the doorway between Dad's room and the rest of my life. There was a din over the apartment, but it seemed like background noise, muffled, far away; everything seemed far away. I caught Terry's eye and said, "I'm not ready for this. I thought I was ready, but I'm not ready yet." I guess Terry hugged me then. I guess he understood.

After some time, a group of us took the elevator down to the lobby. I don't know why we were leaving, going outside; we were taking Mom to someone's house, I think. To Mickey's? She never did return to the apartment. The rest of the evening formed a memory in my mind of something akin to walking through a museum or seeing a remarkable play; some scenes have slipped away from me, and some others are etched permanently onto my heart and will never change or fade away.

One of these sticky memories involves running into Billy Hunt and his colleagues from the funeral home in the doorway. We stood in the foyer holding both doors open, a raucous wind from outside brushing roughly past us, into the building.

I felt startled by the funeral director's vernacular. "We'll take him out tonight; you can stop in tomorrow with some clothes. We got a pickup in the morning, and two cemeteries, then we'll be around. How's 'bout you come by at noon?"

"Where are you taking him? Will he be alone? Will he be cold?" I had so many questions. I, who knew everything about death and dying. I was aware of the winter chill, the silence in the foyer, and my family's forbearance. Training for hospice volunteers pretty much wraps up at the time of death. I had so much more to learn.

"We'll fix him right up tonight," Billy promised. "We'll take good care of your dad." Then, noticing my trembling lip, noticing the others staring, everyone crowded in the icy foyer with the door open and the winter coming in while I thought about what I needed, what they needed, to know, Billy offered, "My dad died almost exactly a year ago."

I tried to wrap my mind around something tangible, something important. Oh, my brain, I thought, this fog, this snow, this damned cold night.

"We'll take good care of him. I'm a friend of your brothers." The poor guy wanted to go inside and get his work done. Yet he waited a moment longer, until I excused him by saying, simply, "Thank you." Dad's family nodded in accord and moved out onto the sidewalk, straight on to everywhere. Oh, Dad. Oh, dear. Oh, no. Who is ever ready to say goodbye?

Not Done

Not done
But gone from here
Kissed goodbye at the gate
Just like that first date
So long ago
But only yesterday
Love knows not the passage of time

-          Sharon

Traditional Irish Blessings

Floating about the universe are hundreds of variations on the traditional Irish Blessing. At an Irish fair, we saw a giant board on which fairgoers were encouraged to write their favorites. The postings ranged from friendly, "May your house be too small to hold all your friends," to hopeful, "May you be in heaven half an hour before the devil knows you're dead."

This one was sent from a time zone away by Erin, not knowing this was exactly the right version. These were precisely our last words to her Grandpa, just hours before.

May the road rise up to meet you,
May the wind be ever at your back
May the sun shine warm upon your face
And the rain fall softly on your fields
And until we meet again,
May God hold you
In the hollow of his hand

Gatekeeper

Gatekeeper
Sitting silently afar
Little voices all call
Many thoughts many minds
Listening from afar
Moments of triumph and defeat
Togetherness
Observing from afar
Surrendering—Accepting
Peacefulness becomes you
Settled in the nest
It's time to rest
Gatekeeper

–   Molly

December 20

Today on a winter walk I prayed
For the first time to my father
Not for him or about him
That's been done plenty
But to him
Because he is again in his place
To protect
To provide
To promote
As he has so often
For so many years
So I prayed
To him
For the first time

-            Terry

Curtains of Night
Will Hayes, 1869

When the curtains of night are
Pinned back by the stars
And the beautiful moon sweeps the skies
When the teardrops of heaven are kissing the rose
It is then that my memory flies

As if on the wings of a beautiful dove
In haste with the message it bears
Just to bring you a kiss of affection and say
"I'll remember you, Love, in my prayers."

So go where you will, on land or on sea
I'll share all your sorrows and cares
And tonight when I kneel by my bedside to pray
I'll remember you, Love, in my prayers.

I have loved you too fondly to ever forget
The love you have spoken to me
And a kiss of affection still warm on my lips
When you told me how true you would be

I know not if fortune be fickle or fair
Or in time will your memory wear
But I know that I love you, wherever you go
And remember you, Love, in my prayers.

When the heavenly angels are guarding the road
As God has ordained them to do
In answer to prayers I have offered above
I know that one's watching o'er you

And may its bright spirit be with you tonight
And guide you up heaven's bright stairs
And be with the one who has loved you so true
And remembers you, Love in my prayers

Part V

Taps

Living On

Longest. Walk. Ever.
Breathless sorrowful parade
Past Dad, one last time.

Left on Lowry

On University Avenue
We forgo the right turn
On 27th
And take a left
On Lowry
For final goodbyes
I feel you on
These old streets
Like a long hard rain
And like a warm light
In every place you
Have been
And in every place
We will ever be
This time
It is a left on Lowry
And straight on
To everywhere

-            Rob

Best. Funeral. Ever.

"Best. Funeral. Ever." Those supportive words made up a text received a few days after we buried Dad. It was followed by a few comments shared over Listserv that filled our hearts with pride and our eyes with tears. Again.

During life's biggest occasions, even when you believe you know what you are doing, someone more experienced, more competent, is always out there, just waiting to teach you how to do whatever you need to do next. After Dad died, before he was buried, our family was surprised and grateful for more experienced voices in our midst: especially the priest, the cemetery staff, and the funeral director.

Billy Hunt, stage manager turned funeral director, apparently arrived on this earth via Central Casting, where he was first understudy for every role ever depicting anyone from the Upper Midwest. Think *Fargo*, the movie. This man was genuine, kind, and almost comically sincere. He was dressed better than some of our guests, and, in a word or two, The Boss. We recommend his services and his family's services to anyone saying goodbye in Minneapolis. He was really good. Which means that, sometimes, he was surprising.

I was put off, at first, by his unscripted, upbeat demeanor and his casual conversations with my brothers, who were old friends of his. This is a deathbed. This is a wake. This is a funeral. Should we not whisper and tiptoe and cry? What are you smiling about? What are you laughing at now? We, as a family, had always allowed for the possibility that we might sidestep a formality or disregard an ordinance if it seemed intended for someone other than us. And yet, in the shadow of this squat, dark-haired Polish guy, we trusted, we obeyed, we followed.

"Family, wait here (directing traffic). You will enter the sanctuary and all proceed past the casket for one last look, then circle around and gather back here in the vestibule. We will then close the casket and begin the funeral service."

Wait. Enter. Proceed. Look. Circle. Gather. Close. How can a simple guy from northeast Minneapolis, with an accent flatter than the ice on Lake Minnetonka, proclaim a few simple words and make hearts step back in surprise, shock, deep and sudden... grief? We were fine until we heard, "Family, we'll take one last look."

I know; Billy Hunt didn't know our dad. But he knew us, and he knew where we were coming from. We were lines on his professional to-do list. And for that list, we were grateful. We are hovering now around numbers 8 or 10 or 12 on that list. Let's say we're at step 10:

10.   Showtime; direct guests to find seats
11.   Direct family to file past casket
12.   Close casket, return jewelry to widow
13.   Family proceeds into sanctuary behind casket
14.   Family folds blanket over casket
15.   Family seated; service begins

We are individuals with minds all our own. But today, we will go where you send us, do as you tell us, and thank you later. We understand interdependence: while planning life's most emotional events (weddings, births, home purchases, ,wisdom teeth, funerals), even when people think they know what they are doing, it can be a good idea to lean on someone who knows a little bit more.

Dad's funeral took place one day after his ninetieth birthday, two days after Christmas, on one of those bright, biting mornings when an icy wind wraps itself mournfully around the corners of the church and everyone steps with some caution across the treacherous sidewalks. Frozen sunlight blasted in through great stained-glass windows, spilling solid colors in patterns across the walls and floor. This was the church where Dad, his parents, and all of his kids started out. This was the church where he worshipped on the day he left for war. It was the right venue. It was a terrible day for a funeral, and everything was perfect.

The funeral started out with a nod to our Irish heritage, a rich rendition of "Danny Boy," followed by Cliff reading from Dad's book, the part about Going Away; the part Mom had commissioned just a week before. Cliff read:

The Essence of Going Away
By Jack Moore

Today is Sunday, January 31st, 1943 and an icy winter wind whistles around the corners of my grandparents' house. I wonder if sometime I might pray to hear that mournful sound again. In less than an hour, I will deliver my future to the United States Army Air Corps. I will go where they send me, do what they tell me, and someday, God willing, be welcomed back to the blare of trumpets and shy smiles from grateful young ladies. However, the date of my return is neither specified nor guaranteed.

Last night, I visited my brothers and my sister at bedtime. It pulled at my heart to say Goodbye instead of Goodnight.

Today, my mother and grandmother and I have risen early and will attend 6 a.m. mass at St. Lawrence Catholic Church, where I was baptized and made my first Communion. We drive there in the dark. The weather is cold and blustery even by the standard of a Minnesota winter.

Six a.m. mass is never very long, and soon the Priest gives us a blessing, and we say a Hail Mary together as he kneels at the front of the altar. We arrive home with enough time for a big breakfast, and a chance to wonder why life has changed so much in such a short time.

Leaving is not going to be as easy as I had pictured it. Mom is biting her lower lip and I know tears will soon be falling. "I'll drive you downtown," she says.

My mother is not happy about the war, and with good reason. Her husband is already in combat and now she must say goodbye to her oldest son. Almost overnight, our family structure has been shattered. The time has come and the condemned man is about to eat a hearty meal, after which he will take a short cab ride to a world he can only imagine. It will be a long time before I enjoy another breakfast like the one my Grandma has just placed before me. Why am I losing my appetite?

I swallow quickly, wash down some bacon with a swig of milk and wade into a battle I don't want to fight. "No, Mom. I'll call a cab. I don't have much to carry. They said to just take the clothes we wear and some toothpaste and stuff."

Grandma quietly clears the table, setting my dishes in the sink. It is not her nature to referee a contest between Mom and me, nor anybody and anybody.

My mother doesn't want to cry. She is dabbing her eyes with a handkerchief, trying to stay strong.

"I want to go down there with you," she cries. "I'm your mother; I want to be with you as long as I can. When will I see you again? Tell me that. Tell me when I'll see your father again. Tell me that."

I don't want to hurt her, but I don't want any long, drawn out goodbyes, either. Now that I'm leaving, I really wish I could stay. But there is no chance of that. Even if I could stay, I would go.

"OK, Mom," I say. "But Grandma goes, too." I look pleadingly at Grandma, who nods in agreement. Mom dries her eyes again, leaves the table and returns wearing her coat.

"All right, let's go," she says plaintively. We hunch against the wind and blowing snow to reach the car.

"I'll drive, Mom," I say, putting my small suitcase into the trunk. I help Grandma into the back seat, hold the door for my mother and climb in behind the wheel of Grandpa's 1938 Plymouth. Mom is in pain, and my leaving is the cause. It is one of those times when there is nothing to say.

As we cross the Mississippi into downtown Minneapolis, the Federal Building becomes visible a few blocks away. Mom is not making things any easier.

"It's not fair," she sobs. "Your father is gone. Why do you have to go, too? I don't want you to go."

I fumble in my mind for something to say. Anything. I don't have to worry. The answer comes from the back seat. It comes in a small but firm voice and the message is clear. I am about to hear a declaration of reality in an unreal world. Grandma has heard enough.

"You stop that right now, Paree. He wants to go. He's a man and he's got a job to do and that's all there is to it. He's going to do what he has to do and you should be proud of it."

My mother stops crying and puts her hand on my shoulder. I turn to glance behind me. Grandma is sitting ramrod straight. She looks me in the eye, smiles, and gives me a wink that goes right to my heart and is still there. God, how I love that woman!

As Cliff read, a person could have heard the sound of that pin everyone is always dropping as it skittered across the sunlit floor.

The service continued with a few verses of "Shall We Gather at the River," followed by that reading about time: A time to be born, a time to die…

Next, we lifted our hearts to sing, "My Lord What a Morning." My Lord, whatta music! Our friends, Mickey's in-laws, Janet and Charles, had blessed countless Moore family occasions with their pipes. On this day, Charles was ill and unable to attend. (During this time, there were so many problems with so many of our fathers, father-in-laws, and others, that Mickey called it the Dadpocolypse.) Janet held her own, of course, but Charles was missed.

Following the music, a reading from Timothy:

The time of my departure is at hand. I have competed well, I have finished the race, I have kept the faith. From now on the crown of righteousness awaits me, which the Lord, the just judge, will award to me on that day, and not only to me, but to all who have longed for his appearance. (2 Timothy 4:7-8)

The gospel advised: Do not let your hearts be troubled. In my Father's house are many rooms. I am going there to prepare a place for you." (John 14:1-4)

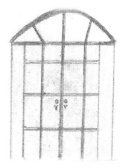

If that's where Dad was going, we could be sure, when each of us arrived, we would find the door unlocked.

Father Bill's homily was memorable. As a reader might deduce, Dad, a radioman, introduced his offspring early to the world of voice recordings and playback buttons. To his delight, the kids grew into talkative, microphone-grappling grownups.

At Dad's wake, each kid took a turn speaking a few words. At the funeral, we capitalized on the fact that Dad was a writer, and we celebrated him by reading his words, not ours, during the service. But the best thing we could have done, the thing we really did right, was to hand the microphone to Dad's friend, the celebrant of his funeral, Father Bill.

The congregation had just found their seats - again and gratefully. The wind had settled down and the colors reaching through the windows had softened. No one knew what would happen next, and that's where Father Bill began.

"I want to talk with Jack's grandchildren," he began. "Will you please stand up?" Up stood all the grandchildren. More than thirty of them, aged prekindergarten to midlife crisis. All were seated with their families, scattered the way movie extras are scattered for a crowd scene—there seemed to be so many of them. They were lovely to look at, all dressed up and all smiling through their sadness. Smiling, because this group was familiar with Father Bill. He'd been around for more than a few family events, and had recently celebrated the funeral of Brian's father-in-law. Brian's kids, in particular, were his buddies. Still are. Sadness, because the members of this faction, to a one, knew that they each were Grandpa Jack's favorite. Dad was a key player in the lives of his grandchildren and they knew it; Father Bill knew it, too. He spoke directly to them:

"How will you honor your grandpa?" Father Bill asked the grands. "Will you honor him by using your talents and your gifts? By loving each other, and by taking care of your grandma?

"There are so many ways to honor your grandpa. When you are driving down the road behind a car traveling too slowly and you see some gray-haired person behind the wheel, don't honk your horn or have road rage toward them. Smile and wave as you pass by. That is how you can honor your grandpa.

"And when you know an old priest is home alone on a Friday night, don't feel sorry for him. Pick him up and take him to the casino. That's what your grandpa would tell you to do.

"That's how you can honor your grandpa. You can be generous and loving and accepting. That is how your grandpa was and that is how he would want you to be. That is how he would want you to honor his memory." Amen.

A Catholic Mass rivals only hatha yoga for up-and-down transitions. After Father Bill spoke, we all rose to offer Prayers of the Faithful, read by the grandchildren:

- We pray for Dad. In baptism he received the light of Christ. Scatter the darkness now and lead him over the waters of death. We pray...
- For friends and loved ones gone before us. Grant them an everlasting home with your Son. We pray...
- Please give comfort and consolation to Mom, who loved Dad and shared fifty-seven years with him. We pray...
- Dad was blessed to receive the support of brave and compassionate caregivers throughout his final days. For those who provide care and comfort to the sick and dying, we pray...

* Dad was a peaceful person, unshakable in his humility. For peace throughout the world, we pray...
* Dad loved to laugh and was quick to smile. May we all find reasons every day to laugh with each other and to share a smile with those around us. We pray...
* Dad was a faithful man. May we learn by his example to know the power of faith in our own lives. We pray...

Rob's daughter, Em, flew into Minnesota from London, via New York City and Appleton, WI. On one of those flights, she picked up laryngitis. On subsequent flights, she drank tea and contemplated the song, "What a Wonderful World," which she hoped to be able to sing at her grandpa's funeral.

Imagine Jimmy Durante or Louis Armstrong on this, singing in hoarse, raspy tones. Now imagine a person their exact opposite: blonde-haired, blue-eyed, twenty-something soprano; a new college graduate but a seasoned singer and professional actress. The voice God gave Em is rich with power and creativity, an incredible gift that had always delighted her grandpa. As he listened to "What a Wonderful World," you can bet he was hollering to the angels, "Hey! Come 'ere! You've gotta hear this!"

Em put considerable thought into her song, and her contemplation found its way into a poem composed in flight.

Fire and Bullets

The sound of the sax in your head
Smoky alto voice in your dreams
Guide you into the fog
Not to worry; someone was waiting for you
She would guide you through the fire
Beautiful music was out there Waiting for you
Records to be played; it was not your time
Fields of green; a calm summer day
An endless line of tees and flags
Games were yet to be played and won
It was not your time
Swarms of people, smiling faces
Your children Their children
Birthdays Easter Christmas
The love of your life would stand by your side
Until your last dying moments
But these trying seconds were not your last
A full and beautiful life was yet to be lived
And the promise of it all Guided you through
The fog The smoke The gunfire
The blinding haze of war
And Carried you home

-        Em

More poetry was on the agenda toward the end of the funeral, including something Dad had written for Mom:

A Most Beautiful Life

Tripping the old light fantastic for me
Was far too much tripping and too little glee.
Slow footed, sluggish and way off the beat
Trampling my partner's unfortunate feet...

Let me help you, I heard, from a voice soft
and breezy.
You can dance. Be yourself, and
the rest will come easy.
All life is a dance, not a game to contest.
We'll just keep it simple and give it our best.

And that's how she taught me to go
One two three.
How just in an instant the world changed for me.
We're flying. We're soaring. I'm king of the ball.
She'll be there to catch me. Who cares if I fall?

One two three. One two three. That's how it goes.
Whirling and spinning and up on your toes.
That was my Emily, that was my wife.
Waltzing me through a most beautiful life.

- Jack Moore

Our final reading came from Dad's book. In the army, each soldier flying a mission in the morning placed a folded white towel at the end of his cot before going to sleep. In the predawn darkness, a soldier walked through the barracks with a flashlight and, catching his light on a white towel, woke that airman with a weighty phrase: "Time to go, Lieutenant." So this is how Dad ended his book. Cliff read:

"Time to Go, Lieutenant."

I have had my wake up call. Today's target will be another world, safer, but much less orderly than you and your friends have known in the last few years. Briefing will be at 1950 hours this evening when you kiss your mother, shake hands with your Father [sic] and hug your brothers and sister. Thank God, it will be over. Your Guardian Angel wishes you good luck and says goodbye.

At the end of a Catholic funeral, the celebrant waves incense over the casket, saying, "May the angels lead you into paradise, may the martyrs come to welcome you and take you to the holy city, the new and eternal Jerusalem."

He then kneels at the foot of the altar, facing the crucifix at the front of the church. He mumbles a few words and then signals for the pallbearers to lead the recession from the church. The parade follows the casket into the winter wind and down the icy steps to where a hearse is waiting. In the background, at Dad's funeral, we heard Janet sing the words that would buoy us through the next days and years, "I'll Be Seeing You."

Taps

Day is done, gone the sun

In the tradition of the United States Military, a US flag drapes the casket of deceased veterans to honor the memory of their service. The flag is placed on a closed casket so the union blue field is at the head and over the left shoulder of the deceased.

From the lakes, from the hills, from the sky

In the tradition of our family, Dad's friends and relatives tromped through the snow together, to a gravesite on a hill overlooking one of the many golf courses Dad had played throughout his lifetime. Cousin Joey fired up his trumpet and claxoned out the long and slow drawl of *Taps*, each note hanging on the bitter winter air until the next note arrived to send it crescendoing home.

All is well

Beside Joey in the snow stood three uniformed military personnel, the Honor Guard. At military funerals, three volleys of shots are fired in honor of a deceased veteran. According to military lore, the three volleys come from an early battlefield custom. Warring sides would recess the conflict to clear the dead and wounded from the battlefield. When the fallen had been cared for, three shots rang out to communicate that the living were ready to resume the battle.

One. The first of the Honor Guards' three gunshots startled people: mothers jumped; children reached for parents' hands. Men watched with interest as the soldiers lowered and again raised their weapons in a single motion.

Two. The second shots shattered the frozen air; husbands stretched arms around wives' shoulders, pulling them close.

Three. The third of the Honor Guards' shots seemed to pierce the crowd itself, triggering quiet tears and drawing the heavily bundled mourners more tightly together. And then, silence.

Safely rest

Under the black branches of an oak tree marking the gravesite, two soldiers ceremoniously folded our American flag into a symbolic tricornered shape. Mom searched the eyes of one of these elegant young men, his dark eyes focused intently on hers alone, making a solemn presentation of the flag. Did she see her husband there?

He said, "On behalf of the President of the United States, the United States Air Force and a grateful Nation, please accept this flag as a symbol of our appreciation for your loved one's honorable and faithful service."

God is nigh

The soldiers marched in unison away from the shivering crowd, descending the snow-covered slope as Father Bill commended Dad's spirit to our Lord.

TAPS

(THE LAST CALL)

Words by H. L. TRIM, Musician Prescott Post No. 1, G. A. R.

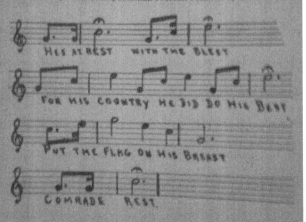

HES AT REST   WITH THE BLEST

FOR HIS COUNTRY HE DID DO HIS BEST

PUT THE FLAG ON HIS BREAST

COMRADE   REST

RESPECTFULLY DEDICATED TO OUR
DEPARTED COMRADES

The Rite of Committal

Christians believe the grave is sacred, a place blessed to hold an artifact of great value: the body of someone awaiting Christ's return to Earth. With this in mind, the grave is blessed this way:

> Lord Jesus Christ, by your own three days in the tomb, you hallowed the graves of all who believe in you and so made the grave a sign of hope that promises resurrection even as it claims our mortal bodies. Grant that our brother may sleep here in peace until you awaken him to glory.

Finally, Dad's body was entrusted to the earth and his soul entrusted to God:

> Because God has chosen to call our brother from this life to Himself, we commit his body to the earth, for we are dust and unto dust we shall return. Let us commend our brother to the Lord, that the Lord may embrace him in peace and raise up his body on the last day. Eternal rest grant unto him, oh Lord, and may perpetual light shine upon him. May he rest in peace. Amen.

After a brief silence, Billy Hunt, our emcee/funeral director broke the meditative spell looming over us, clapping his gloved hands together and announcing, "That concludes our service." Did he say? "You've been a great audience! We're here every Saturday!" No, but he did say, "You may each take a flower to remember him by."

A flower? A flower? What about a simple red flower would remind us of the man we are burying today? This man, who earned a Purple Heart and donned a purple snowmobile suit, wore yellow golf shirts and plaid pants for eighteen holes on Saturday mornings and cribbage on Saturday afternoons, who stood at the glass by the blue line at hockey games holding a cup of black coffee? What about a red flower would remind us of anything at all? Except that in three days, that flower would be dead, and our dad would be dead, as well. Seriously? A flower?

And with that question top of mind, we acquiesced (look it up), stripping green stems and scarlet blossoms from a bouquet of carnations and roses that were jammed into a planter set in the snow beside the casket. While we made our selections, Dad waited patiently to be lowered into the frozen earth.

I lifted a red carnation close to my lips, inhaled its frozen fragrance and exhaled. Then, looking down only at the sullied snow, without a firm plan in my mind, I leaned into the wind and pushed further uphill, to where I knew other family members had been laid to rest. Great-grandparents, grandparents, an uncle still living, a brother, an infant representing the many infant deaths among us—they all have places there. The gravestones had been cleared of snow and their engraved lettering shimmered under the exhausted winter light.

Without a word, I dropped my flower on the stone plate shared by my brother and my son. From behind, I felt my husband's hand on my shoulder, and saw his red carnation drop down beside mine, and then someone else dropped another and then, someone else, another. And gradually the bouquet gathered itself back together, a gift connecting Dad to his People so acutely that, going forward, every red rose or carnation would forever after remind us of our dad, and his People, and goodbye.

Epilogue

Blessings in the End

"This is life," anyone will say.
But I am not settled with that.
Not yet.

Blessings in the End

Rain in Ohio
Tears so many states away
I'll never forget

My heart aches for one heart, half of the two
who created us all. Part of me wishes to share
their embrace. Mostly there's comfort that so
many others are there. I'm one rain drop, loved,
missed. Loss brought us together.

-    Paree

As I write this last section, we are coming up on the first anniversary of Dad's moving on. We have moved on, too, as well as we know how.

We had a party on Dad's birthday last year, and have plans to continue that longstanding tradition again this December twenty-sixth.

We made it through that first Easter without Dad on hand to hide the Family Egg. The Family Egg? It is a hardboiled, creatively colored real egg with the names of all of the children and grandchildren and great-grandchildren intertwined, the letters necessarily getting smaller year after year. Sometime during 2014, we will have two Moore names to add to the Family Egg, and likely more after that.

We made it through Mom and Dad's anniversary, a few high school graduations, a medical school graduation, and a wide range of concerts, plays, and sporting events Dad would have been proud to attend.

We made it through Thanksgiving, too. But the cold wind and the browning of the world are icy reminders of where we were a year ago, the day of the doctor's visit, the day of the Hospice Intake Meeting, the day an otherwise friendly physician said to my mother, "Two to four days."

Rob says the drive from Appleton to Minneapolis is tough these days, as he remembers the phone conversations he was having during the same drive at this time last year. He remembers Mickey asking when he'd be back, and he laughs when he recalls that he was already halfway to Minneapolis when she asked. But it's a sad laughter, and kind of empty, because there's no satisfaction in a punch line like that.

I agree with Rob about the drive. Coming from Detroit to Minneapolis this fall, I was reminded, unexpectedly, that a certain Oasis is where I was putting gas in the car when Mickey called to say, "Hurry!" And that curve in the freeway near Madison is where we were when they put Dad on the phone, just in case. Then, somewhere near Tomah, Paree called about the black ice in St. Paul. To me, there has always been something sinister about the trees losing their leaves, about the world dropping all expression to become only gritty, brown and gray, and cold. Memories just compound that sensation.

Of course, there have been blessings, too. Dad would want us to see them. He would want us to appreciate the upside of things. The joy Mom is finding in new friendships, puzzles, card games, cross-country travel, and book after book after book—it's a lovely thing. She'd trade it all to have him back, I know, but he always looked out for her happiness, and still seems to be doing so. One of the most profound gifts a father can give his children is to love their mother. Thanks, Dad, for that.

Following are some of the notes and updates that showed up on Listserv over this past year. Dad wanted us to stay together and to take care of Mom. I think we've accomplished that.

This Listserv conversation is characteristic. It began as a plea to the siblings to join forces to help Mom write some thank-you notes. It rapidly traveled in other directions.

From: Lindy
Sent: Saturday, January 19, 11:39 AM
Subject: Thank you night

I have the picture boards from the funeral here. I sent Mom's photo books with Pen. Thought she might be missing them. I didn't see Dad's book in with this stuff, though. Does anyone know who has Mom's copy of Dad's book? I also still have shirts.

Dad's voice is in my head today. Does anyone else get that? Just the tone of his voice.

Okay, I'm sad now. I will be taking a dysfunctional day today. Plan on watching TJ play hockey tonight on Fox.

From: Rob
Sent: Saturday, January 19, 12:08 PM
Subject: Re: Thank you night

Yeah, Lindy, Dad's voice has been in my head, too. Not really a voice as much as a presence. I told Mickey I woke up the other day and had a clear vision stuck in my head. It wasn't something I had thought about in a long time, if ever. It was a few of us sitting around the kitchen table with Mom and Dad. We had gone there to surprise Dad with the news that we had nominated him for the Hall of Fame and he had been accepted. He cried when we told him. I thought this vision was him reminding me that we had done things that made him happy and proud, to remember him being grateful for us, and not focusing so much on the sadness, grief and perpetual pit in the stomach when we realize each day that he is gone.

Then, last Sunday at mass, I found myself transfixed by the familiar cadence of the ritual and appreciating the surprising vocal quality of the singer. Then, I heard the priest read the line, "You are my beloved son, in whom I am well pleased." I looked at John and he smiled and winked. We both heard it the same way. Obviously, Dad did not write or speak that line. But it was something Dad would say now, to all of us, so that's how it felt at that moment.

Like all of us, I always enjoy talking to Mom. But I appreciate it in a different way now. Their voices were always such a sweet duet. I am thankful I can still hear one of those artists who made that music with their voices. I realize I will never forget his voice as long as I can hear hers. That's how close they were, and are still, in my head and heart.

Anyway, thanks for letting me ramble. I miss you guys. Who woulda thought that old folks home would have become such a memory of home for me, when I think of all of you, and those last few weeks?

From: Julie
Sent: Saturday, January 19, 6:54 PM
Subject: RE: Thank you night

I don't have any voices. I have Dad's photo on my phone, and that catches me off guard sometimes. But not hearing him?

Mom's demeanor is cheerful and she is open about her sadness when it strikes. We talk a lot about Dad and sifted through his medals box this morning. The phone rings off the hook and she really smiles when it does—she is so happy to have every call and conversation. I know people worry that she is lonely, but she doesn't say so. She is giving me lessons in grieving.

Is It Like Losing a Limb?

Is it like losing a limb?
When your best friend leaves
And you are left standing
One handed
Holding only your breath,
Is it like losing a limb?

Is it like a heart stopping?
When your soul mate fades from view
And you are left with only a pillow to
Clutch against your chest,
Is it like a heart stopping?

Is it like shadows gathering?
When your light fades from view
And you are left sorting photos
Blurred through watery eyes,
Is it like shadows gathering?

Is it like reaching?
Let our arms wrap around you,
The stone in your chest become ours to carry,
The shadows clear away so we can see
The vibrant memories all around us.
Can you reach? Can you feel us here?

\-   Julie

Sailing

When I reflect on Dad's hospice days, I picture sailing in the middle of an ocean. There were hours of turbulence (weathering the storm) and hours of so much calm (sailing with the breeze under a cloudless blue sky). Peace and discord. Those days were both terrible and wonderful. Each hour stretched into eternity and yet all were collectively too short. That is how I think of those days, our last days with our dad.

What do I remember? Everything, yet nothing. I know that every word was spoken between Dad and me that could be said, but was it enough? Funny, my takeaways are much the same as any visit anytime with Dad. Watching him enjoy the Vikings game, hugs, I love you's, got to play that music, get that radio station started. Feeling the confidence he instills in me; how is that different from any other day?

What I find remarkable is his quiet acceptance of his mortality, his ability to let us crowd him with affection and helping hands, smiling and offering us glimpses of his unique humor. Without a doubt, Dad knew he was loved and we knew he loved us. Without a doubt, it was Dad's time to leave us for the heavens, but that is little comfort when I realize my dad is not going to be there for a quick visit, or a bucket of balls at the golf course, or to coax into a movie at the Heights Theater.

I know he was blessed with a peaceful goodbye, surrounded by his People, embraced by his beloved wife; but I am still so sad, a little for him, but mostly for all of us and especially for Mom. A blessing and a curse. "This is life," anyone will say. But I am not settled with that. Not yet.

-     Mary

Tag

I woke in the middle of the night to play tag with Sleep... again. This is common over the past few weeks and sleep always seems to have the upper hand. So while I chase the elusive Sleep I begin to think. This is how Sleep keeps me down. I think of my dad and my life—another common occurrence. I note all the stupid things I have done. Some selfish, immature and most just plain STUPID. I wonder if he has forgiven me.

My mind drifts to his hugs at the top of the stairs. The way his eyes would light up and the big smile when I walked into his apartment. The kiss when he was so weak but still lifted his head and arms with an embrace. He loves me. Forgive me? He didn't need to. He probably never thought about those things again. He loves me unconditionally.

I brush off the tears, roll over and pull the covers up under my chin. I say to Sleep, "Tag, you're it."

- Sharon

Winter on Lake of the Isles

It might seem to someone reading Listserv that we are entombed in our grief because so much of what we share is on this topic and so few of us wax poetic about the great deal Mom got on avocados, or about the avocado cupcakes we made the next day. Admittedly, life marches ahead. But I appreciate knowing that when life pauses for a moment to let sadness have its voice, there is a Listserv littered with souls who understand. That said, here is my moment for today:

I cannot walk and weep at the same time
Because my tears freeze into puddles
On the sidewalk and I lose my footing
So many broken winter hearts
We force our faces into the wind and spill tears
Across the parking lot as we race
To erase lines on a task list
Leaving glaze ice in unnatural places
We slip and fall unexpectedly
On a thin frozen layer of grief
We cannot stumble now
We must hold each other steady
We must lace up our CCMs
And skate over this impossible time
Until the blue jay bids the sun come out
Until the jackets change
Until the tears stream into the ocean and away

-   Julie

Entombed

In a way, I do feel entombed in grief. I wake up missing my dad, praying to him and talking to him all day, every day. I keep busy, but at different times the tears burn behind my eyes like a small child, lost. But we go on. I am different now—better or worse? I don't know—just different. Anyway, thank you Listserv because, with all of you, I know I am not crazy!

-   Sharon

Or was she? Grief can cause a person to question his or her bearings. I was beginning to question mine, as, over the phone one afternoon, Sharon chirped lightheartedly about the conversations she has with Dad. She started, "When Dad and I were talking yesterday__"

I had to interrupt to ask, "You talk to him?"

"Sure."

"He answers?"

"Of course." Like, you eat guacamole with those chips? Or, you separate your reds from your whites in the laundry? Sure. Of course.

I checked in with my daughter Kasey, who has skeptic DNA. "Grandpa never talks to me. Should I be jealous? Or is Sharon crazy?"

Kasey was characteristically supportive. "I suppose, a little of both."

I turned to Mom, who, as a grieving widow, was allowed to be a little crazy, although she stayed mostly levelheaded. "Does Dad ever talk to you, like, with words?"

"Well," Mom hesitated, but she can never tell a lie. "No. But I talk to him." Ah, ha! Sharon was HALF crazy.

I told Mom, "I don't have any voices. I think about him, but, not hearing him? What does that mean?"

Mom smiled the way all mothers smile when they do love their children but want to know what puts these paranoid ideas into their tiny, worked-up minds. That look was the only answer she could provide. It was enough.

Mostly

Mostly you are not insane
Merely unimpressed
Merely different from the rest
You are unimpressed

Mostly you are not to blame
For the raging sky
For the tumult where you fly
Let it pass you by

Mostly what you see is not yours
Do not claim it
Do not, for the life of you, own it

'cause mostly you are not insane
Merely unrefined
Merely free and undefined
Confused, perhaps, but keep in mind
Thunder passes with the rain
And mostly
You are not
Insane

- Rob

Play On

I like how Grandpa makes his way back to remind us
he is watching. A guy in a cube across the hall plays
jazz pretty quiet that Grandpa would like. After
working there a month I asked him about it and he
was shocked I could hear it. Refreshing.

You know, I was thinking about when Grandpa told
Molly and me, "I chose you" (meaning all of us). I
wonder sometimes if it was God who was talking (in a
sense) through Grandpa. Because, at the end of the
day, God chose Grandpa to be ours, too. Grandpa
seemed to express that he chose us particularly. We
were chosen. It was an honorable moment. Many
people have shown me how to be strong, intelligent
and loving; but Grandpa and Grandma have done so
in their own way and that moment made it clear,
again, that Grandpa loves us.

I've been reminded of him often during this stressful
time in my life. I've been blessed with rare, good jazz
radio on my long drives. My friend at school said her
dad mixes hot chocolate and cinnamon with his coffee
and calls it a Cadillac. It made me smile. What a
delicious sounding drink to go along with the word
that always reminds me of Grandpa.

-   Anna

Love Abounds

It surrounds me
Fills the spaces and isn't spring lovely
From gray to green
We skipped a step
Not knowing that big rock
In the center of everything
Just gets in the way
We sat there a long while
Stringing toes in the water
Counting seconds minutes days
And then we wandered
Away
One or two at a time
We stepped off quietly
On our own
Setting down in the river
A splash, a ripple, a turn to the sun
A bow and a wave
Then we set out
Laying back
Feet first to the current
Palms up
Till it spun us around
To the deep
Blue
Sea

-      Penny

Her Time

It is time
To prepare for her journey
Her own journey
Her own
But not alone
He is there in the distance
Watching, protecting, guiding, as always.
We are here
Her People, his People
Their People
Catering, caring, supporting
Still it is
Her journey to take
Where she will...
So we pack and sort
Through 57 years
We move and prepare
For her journey.
Always knowing he is there
In the distance.

- Sharon

Something Irish

when ye notice the tide
on an inbound ride
with ye there alone
in the sand
then some other voice
and not by yer choice
will bid ye be tall
where ye stand

'tis the voice that you hear
not loud and not clear
that begs ye to know
this shall pass
waters raging at rocks
breaking dams, ships and docks
shall bend not a blade of your grass

when the storm that approaches
no longer encroaches
then some other voice
shall say
the tide too recedes
see—
yer troubles and needs
are now out to sea and
away

-   Rob

the tide, too, recedes…

Author's Note

F. Scott Fitzgerald wrote that the world looks better when observed through a single window. I wouldn't know. I have lived all my life in a kaleidoscope; this book is one view, one perspective, one turn of the tube on a scene that involved countless windows, countless moving parts. If you ask someone else, they will say, "Hold that thing up to the light! Look!" The beads fall differently for each of us.

I wish to thank my siblings for allowing me this view. I appreciate everyone's contributions and I hope they will continue to add their colors to this story over time. If you, reader, wish for another perspective, ask someone who was there: Grandma Emy, Mary, Jay, Lindy, Penny, Rob, Terry, Mickey, Sharon, Chris, Brian, and their families.

Special thanks to Anne Myers-Richards, Volunteer Coordinator, Fairview Homecare and Hospice, for guidance. Thanks to the Vixens for support, to Cathy Vennewitz for design, to Miriam Queensen and Alison Baker for editing, and to Adrianne Hamilton-Butler for asking tough questions, such as, "Who cares?"

Thank you, above all, to my husband, Jack, for living alongside me in the kaleidoscope, and to my children, Erin, Matteson, Patrick, Matthew, Maureen, and Kasey Anne for your vibrant colors and views. Everything I do is for you. Sorry more of what I do is not laundry.

Finally, this book is for families. Protect Families.

Thanks.

Resources

For excellent resources, including links to related services as well as information on connecting with hospice organizations in your area, please refer to the **National Hospice and Palliative Care Organization, www.NHPCO.org**

In *Hospice Isn't a Place*, we meet Jack Moore at the time of his cancer diagnosis. Jack also lived with Alzheimer's disease. His family leaned heavily on their local chapter of the Alzheimer's Association and were positively impacted by the resources they found there: **www.ALZ.org.**

The Author and the Moore Family are available to meet with your class, group, or family to share hospice stories and experiences. Please visit the website for contact information:

www.HospicePeople.org

Medical Disclaimer

The author is not responsible or liable, directly or indirectly, for any damages whatsoever resulting from the use or misuse of information presented here. This publication is designed to provide general information about hospice care, death, and dying, as our family experienced it. It was written and is distributed with the understanding that the author is not a licensed medical professional.

While extensive effort has been made to provide accurate information, every family should engage the services of qualified and competent care professionals during every hospice journey.

Hospice Isn't a Place; It's People

Conversation Starters

Part I: Hospice Isn't a Place

1. What is your experience with death and dying?
2. Do you remember the first funeral you attended? Who died? How did you find out? Who accompanied you to the funeral?
3. What ideas did you have at that time about dying? Has your perspective changed over time?
4. Planning ahead and completing certain legal documents can be helpful at the end of life. Have you thought through your own last wishes? Who knows what your wishes are?
5. "Bless Us, Oh, Lord" implores the reader to respect the dying person's beliefs. Do you agree? Why or why not?

Part II: Something You Carry With You

6. Family relationships are complex. Which of your own family relationships do you view as strongest? Which are more strained?
7. The author suggests that adults have a responsibility to parent themselves. If you could parent yourself as a child, what would you do in the same way? What would you do differently?
8. Brian explores the idea of ending life "Satisfied." How does he propose one arrives at Satisfied? Do you agree?
9. Dad's wartime experience was both transforming and also completely separate from his life before and after the

war. How did this experience shape him? How might it have influenced his end-of-life experience?

Part III: Our Hospice Story

10. Dad chose not to undergo the surgery that might have extended his life. Why did he make this choice? Why do you think his family went along with it?

11. Are some ways of dying more acceptable than others?

12. Emily set the tone for the Hospice Intake Meeting. How did she do this? Why?

13. Once hospice care had begun, the family was faced with a string of decisions. Describe some of the decisions people made, and how those decisions might have helped or hurt the situation.

14. Food is a significant component of our culture today. How did attitudes about food affect decisions and discussions about Dad's care?

Part IV: Actively Dying

15. Have you been present at a death? What happened? How did that affect you?

16. Read aloud Mother Teresa's quote about making sacrifices. What sacrifices did this family have to make? Why did they do this?

17. Palliative or comfort care works in tandem with medication for pain relief. Discuss some of these methods. Can you think of others? How do you apply these techniques in your life outside of hospice care?

18. A serious conflict arose between the family and one of the nurses working in Dad's assisted-living residence.

What were the dynamics at work there? What would you have done?

19. Dad said goodbye to his family in a variety of ways. Are there people you would like to have beside you when you die? What would you say to them?

20. Read the poem "Winter Birds" aloud. What is this poem about?

21. Before he died, Dad said he "had to go." He said he had "things to do." What do you think happens after death, if anything?

22. After Dad died, the author describes feeling "not ready." How can this be? Have you ever found yourself in a comparable situation?

Part V: Taps

23. This section of the book describes Dad's funeral and burial in some detail. How did this sendoff differ from those you have experienced? Have you preplanned your own funeral or service? With whom have you shared your plans? Has your vision of this event evolved over time?

Epilogue: Blessings in the End

24. The topic of this book, of course, is hospice: death and dying and illness and loss. Why do you think the author chose this title, Blessings, as her final word on the subject?

25. In the poem, "Living Without a Limb," the author imagines what her mother, Emily, might be experiencing as a grieving widow. What do you think Emily might be feeling at this point?

26. Read "Love Abounds." What images does this poem bring to mind? What emotions does the poem evoke when you hear it read aloud?

27. Read "Something Irish" aloud. How does this poem mirror the book as a whole?

28. In the Author's Note, the author states that hers is only one view. Why do you think it is important for her to make this statement?

66083747R00140

Made in the USA
Charleston, SC
09 January 2017